No Pictures in My Grave

No Pictures in My Grave

A SPIRITUAL JOURNEY IN SICILY

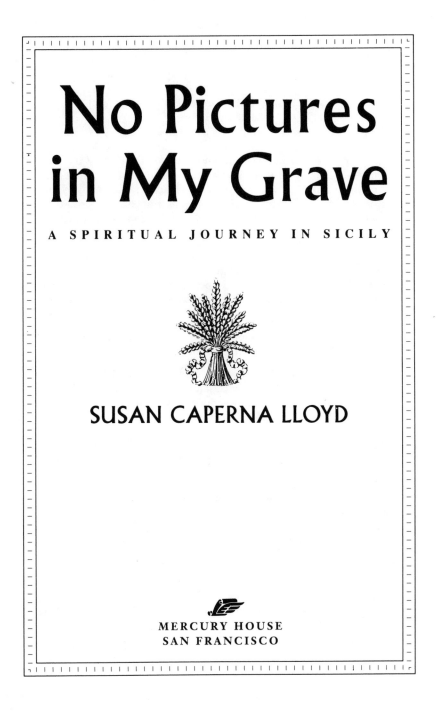

SUSAN CAPERNA LLOYD

MERCURY HOUSE
SAN FRANCISCO

Published in the United States by
Mercury House
San Francisco, California

United States Constitution, First Amendment: Congress shall make no law respecting an establishment of religion, or prohibiting the free exercise thereof; or abridging the freedom of speech, or of the press; or the right of the people peaceably to assemble, and to petition the Government for a redress of grievances.

Mercury House and colophon are registered trademarks
of Mercury House, Incorporated

Photo on page viii courtesy of Susan Caperna Lloyd;
all other photos by Susan Caperna Lloyd.
Text designed by Zipporah W. Collins
Printed on acid-free paper
Manufactured in the United States of America

Library of Congress Cataloging-in-Publication Data

Lloyd, Susan Caperna.
  No pictures in my grave: a spiritual journey in
Sicily / by Susan Caperna Lloyd.
    p. cm.
  ISBN 1-56279-023-4
  1. Sicily (Italy)—Religious life and customs. 2.
Self-realization—Religious aspects. 3. Lloyd, Susan
Caperna. I. Title.
BL980.I8L56   1992
291.4'0945'8—dc20   91-35598
                                                              CIP

5 4 3 2 1

TO MY MOTHER

In memory of Grandmother Carolina

Contents

Carolina Caperna and her children, Amelia, Romy, and Gino; Rome, 1922.

Dear Grandmother Carolina,

I remember the story of how Antonio died in your arms; Dad called me up at college one day to tell me what he'd heard from Uncle Gino, who had been there.

"You know, Susan," said Dad, "Pop got up in the middle of the night and had a heart attack in the bathroom. Mom rushed in, picked him up, and sat on the edge of the bathtub, holding him. 'Antonio, don't die,' she said."

Then I heard Dad crying on the other end of the phone. "You know what Gino said?" he continued. "He said that when he came in and saw Pop dying in her arms like that, it was like the Pietà. It was a damn Pietà. She was like some great Virgin—you know how strong Mom was—holding her son, Jesus."

All your life you were a grieving Madonna and long-suffering mother. You protected your sons and guided your husband into the grave. But how could anyone bear the world's sorrows in that way? Who protected you?

Even with your own death, the nurturing didn't stop. I remember Dad's story of your funeral, which he flew back to New Jersey to attend.

"Mom looked beautiful in death, Susan," he said. "I took a picture of me and your brother, Gary, out of my wallet and placed it in the coffin. This way, she'll pray for us . . . Gary and I are going to need it."

Why did Dad forget to put a picture of me and my sisters in your grave? I guess he thought we were already strong, like you. But sometimes I feel I need protecting. What a load for you to bear, Carolina. At the least, your burden should be lighter. How else can you, or any of us, rise up and be free? I hope that I will have no sad tears, no pictures in my grave.

CHAPTER I

Processione

THE TALL YOUNG WOMAN looked around helplessly, then threw herself to the ground, jarring the people out of their festival mood. With a black cape pulled about her face, she portrayed Mary convincingly as, with growing hysterics, she beat the ground with her fists. Ahead of her in the procession, though she did not see him, was her "son," Christ, wearing a bloodied mask and chained to two men dressed as Roman soldiers. He had just been sentenced to death and was being led off to his crucifixion.

"Where's my son?" cried the woman, her eyes searching through the crowd.

She got up and ran along the street, while crying women in the crowd reached out to comfort her. It was difficult to separate rite from reality in this annual Holy Thursday Passion Play in Marsala, Sicily. I had only expected a quiet religious parade or a simple drama when I had arrived that morning via the northwest coast road from Trapani, where I was staying.

A sharp March wind blew in from the sea, whipping the cape tightly around the woman playing Mary. I couldn't take my eyes off her as she passed by, just inches away. Why did she look so familiar? Then I realized that her proud face reminded me of my dad's mother, Carolina, an Italian immigrant. Grandmother had been a large-boned woman, almost six feet tall, with the same strong yet tragic face. I also remembered another likeness, one I had seen a few days before, gazing out at me from the glass cases in the archaeological museum in Agrigento, south of Marsala. But that image was 2,500 years old. It was a bust of Demeter, a Greek agricultural goddess who had been imported to Sicily and southern Italy well before 500 B.C. I had seen hundreds of terra-cottas of this imposing deity in Sicilian museums. In every piece, Demeter's statuesque body and stern, serious face had conveyed some psychic quality that she shared with my grandmother and with the distraught Madonna I now watched in Marsala's play.

I shouldn't have been surprised. Demeter, too, was a hysterical mother. She had lost her daughter, Persephone, who had been abducted by the god of the underworld, Pluto. According to the Italian version of the myth, Persephone was picking wildflowers on the shore of Sicily's Lake Pergusa when Pluto, in a horrifying moment, had appeared in his chariot and taken her down into Hades. Demeter had watched helplessly from her temple above the lake. Donning a black cape, she had begun a long search for her child and, in revenge, had damned Sicily to eternal winter.

"Spring will not return until I find Persephone," she vowed.

The fertile land had turned black, matching Demeter's raven cloak. She had searched through nine long days and nights. Eventually she found her daughter, only to discover that Persephone had become Pluto's bride. But the wily Demeter bargained with Pluto, and he allowed Persephone to return for spring and summer. Still, because she had eaten the six pomegranate seeds with which he had tempted her, he could command that she come back to him for fall and winter. Thus, with Persephone's yearly wintertime descent and subsequent springtime resurrection, the seasons had come to Sicily, and for centuries following, fertility rites to ensure crop regrowth had been performed in her and her mother's honor.

I thought of this as I watched the distraught Madonna in Marsala, now a block away from me and wailing loudly with her hands in the air. She was a far cry from the Madonnas I had grown up with in my Italian Catholic girlhood. Those Virgins were delicate statues of porcelain or graceful schoolbook illustrations with modest blue robes and sweet, ivory-colored faces. They were gentle creatures, the kind Grandmother Carolina had prayed to. But this Marsala Madonna was different. She was dark and angry. She was powerful and struck me as more like Demeter than Mary. Could Christ, then, be another version of Persephone? Grandmother would have been appalled! But it wasn't so farfetched. After all, one of Persephone's names, in the early Greek language, meant "savior."

But now, here in Marsala, Christ was definitely male. In fact, there were three more versions of him in the play, each of them wearing masks with decidedly masculine beards poking out. As they stumbled along in the milelong procession, they were oblivious to the staring crowd. The masks with their frozen expressions separated the men from the surrounding profane world; instead, they seemed to be in a sacred netherworld with Christ. The last man carried a cross while, behind him, another wailing Madonna was comforted by actors playing Mary Magdalene and Saint John. This Madonna's demeanor, like Demeter's, was wild and passionate. She and her two attendants moved against a background of fields of tender wheat shoots, which were just visible on Marsala's outskirts. I followed this group for several blocks, entranced.

Suddenly a hand touched my shoulder. It was Carlo

Sugameli, a friend from Trapani. I had met Carlo five years before on my first visit to Sicily, when I had spent Holy Week in Trapani. Carlo was a tall, good-looking Sicilian; he had learned to speak English while working as an engineer on American oil ships in the Persian Gulf and Indian Ocean. Today he had driven me the twenty miles from Trapani to Marsala.

"Where have you been? We must go to Trapani," he scolded. "It's time to decorate the *Misteri*." He pushed through the crowd and stepped up onto the sidewalk, motioning for me to follow.

We walked several blocks looking for his car; finally we found it and then moved at a snail's pace through the traffic. Carlo was distracted and edgy. Tomorrow was Good Friday, when Trapani's own Holy Week rite, the four-hundred-year-old Procession of the Mysteries, would be held. In it Carlo, as a *portatore*, or porter, would help carry one of nineteen immense statues through Trapani's streets for twenty-four hours. These statues, the *Misteri*, had been sculpted by Trapani artisans in the sixteenth century, and they depicted figures from the Passion story. They were beloved icons to the Trapanesi; kept in the Church of the Purgatory, they now awaited their annual adornment of flowers and silver ornaments. I knew how important this ritual was to Carlo, but in my fascination with Marsala's play, I had forgotten the time.

The traffic thinned and Carlo raced northward along the highway. In our silence, I looked out the window at acres of green wheat trembling in the wind; the fields were an enduring link to Demeter and Persephone. I thought of Sicily's Greek colonizers, who had revered these deities, and of how, after the Roman era, the worship of them had died out in the ensuing tide of conquest and Christianization. Poised strategically in the Mediterranean, midway between Gibraltar and Constantinople, the island had always been a magnet for invaders: through the centuries,

Phoenicians, Greeks, Carthaginians, Romans, Normans, Byzantines, Arabs, and more had come here. When the Spanish arrived in the sixteenth century, their culture and religion had quickly taken root. Feasts for the saints and Holy Week celebrations had sprung up in every town. But the old deities weren't entirely dead. The Sicilians, inheriting their ancestors' fertility rites, had simply transferred their worship to the saints and to another dying and resurrecting god, Christ.

Carlo and I drove through a little town where bloodied lambs and rabbits hung in butcher-shop windows waiting to be purchased for the upcoming Easter feast. Closer to Trapani, to our left along the sea, was a marshy area striped by the silvery bands of salt flats. An occasional windmill created a scene out of *Don Quixote*. Then, up ahead, loomed the mountain fortress of Erice where the remains of a Greek temple to Aphrodite stood; below the abutment was the promontory of Trapani, curving out to sea on Sicily's westernmost tip. The word *Trapani*, curiously, denoted the black strip of cloth hung on Sicilian doorways to announce a death or funeral. In the distance I could see the whitewashed Moorish-style buildings of Trapani's Old Town; today they were more celestial than funereal in the glistening late-afternoon light.

I spotted the baroque dome of the Church of the Purgatory, sandwiched among tile roofs and the spires of other churches. It was here, among the *Misteri*, that the *Madonna Addolorata* stood waiting. She was the Mother of Sorrows, a statue of the dark-faced Madonna who was carried last in the procession. I remembered the first time I had seen her, five years before.

I had come to Trapani with my husband and young son after visiting Dad's relatives in Terracina, just south of Rome. There I had hoped to find my "roots," the relatives on Carolina's side of the family who'd remained behind in Italy. Carolina had been a strong influence during my childhood, and understanding her and the meaning of "family" had become my obsession. In America, though my dad's Italian mores upset me at times, I was fascinated by our ties. I battled against his expectations of me, yet I felt compelled to search his family out, even to the Mediterranean. But I had found only disappointment in Terracina. The relatives had been distant and indifferent; I wondered if they weren't still angry at Carolina for leaving Italy. I felt rejected. Looking for an escape, and since it was almost Easter, we had decided to take the train and ferry to Sicily. I also had an ulterior motive. As a photographer and writer, I suspected that a Sicilian Easter Week would provide me with interesting and colorful story material.

We had arrived in Trapani on Palm Sunday and the townspeople had welcomed us with open arms. Perhaps because tourists were rarer here than on the mainland, they seemed flattered that we had come. We met several *portatori* who escorted us around the town, insisting we stay for the procession. We had, and it was then that I realized, while viewing the procession's pageantry and spectacle, that I did have a fantastic story. But more important, it was then that I had seen the *Madonna Addolorata* for the first time. Carried on a platform, she was at the long procession's very end, bobbing woefully along. The procession seemed to focus on her: searching for her son, she had been greeted with bravos and tears. At that point, the story I wanted to tell became a personal one. I recognized something of my grandmother in this powerful though sorrowful Madonna, and I became determined to understand the long-suffering nature of Italian women's lives. How was it that in Sicily the focus of the whole town was not on the dying son but on the grief-struck mother?

Trapani's sickle shape was now a dark shadow in the dying purple light. As Carlo drove onto the peninsula, I reflected on the Madonna's upcoming somber task. Perhaps the town's "black cloth" name was appropriate.

Tomorrow there would be another funeral procession in Trapani. And the Madonna, escaping the confines of the church, would come out, looking once more for her son.

Drawn back to Sicily to witness this search again, I had come with Tom and our two sons, Sky, who was now nine, and Shane, almost four. I felt like a returning pilgrim, over-joyed to see the Trapanesi again. But as welcomed as we were, I still struggled with the Mediterranean culture, its language and sometimes alien customs. Though I now considered the Trapani community a family, I was still the *americana* to them, a woman being toured about by males` like Carlo in a society where, I was fast discovering, a woman's proper place was at home.

During this trip I had tried to meet Trapani's women. I had seen them in the churches lighting votive candles or saying rosaries—like my grandmother, who had attended mass daily. Or I had caught glimpses of them hanging out the wash on apartment balconies, festooned with strings of garlic. They had cast furtive glances at me as they bought vegetables from a street vendor or hurried to the fish mar-ket. But mostly they stayed inside, unseen; I imagined them huddled over pots of steaming spaghetti. I remem-bered Carolina in her grease-smeared apron; all her life, the kitchen had been her world. This was the place where, even in the face of tremendous poverty, she could nurture her family. Were these Trapani women like her? Did they have their Antonios who sat melancholy in the kitchen corners, as my grandfather had when he grew old, reliving the past and watching Mama cook?

I'd had no luck. The women were invisible. I had learned that many of their sons—men like Carlo, who was in his midthirties—still lived at home. It seemed sacrosanct, the inside life of the family. I had been both impressed with and annoyed at Carlo's allegiance to this institution. Every day like clockwork, Carlo would phone home from the lo-cal bar where we would all meet to drink espresso. He was

calling to check on his mother and to find out when he was
expected for the midday meal, *la cena.*

Carlo and I sped through Trapani's New Town, a hodge-
podge of modern buildings hastily erected in the 1950s
after the devastating bombings of World War II. We continued to the peninsula's very tip. Here, the streets were con-
voluted and narrow, barely allowing cars to pass. We
parked next to the Pensione Messina, where my family and
I were staying. I knew that Tom and the boys wouldn't be
back yet from their day trip to Palermo, so Carlo and I hurried over to the Church of the Purgatory.

The *Madonna Addolorata* stood just to the left inside the
church doors as several *portatori* scurried about below her.
One had climbed up on the *ceto,* or platform, on which she
stood, and he was dressing her in a black satin cape. Another stood eagerly below, holding an antique silver heart
stabbed with seven daggers that represented the sorrows
Mary had experienced. This man handed the heart up to
the one on top, while a lone middle-aged woman, standing
below and consulting a photo from last year's procession,
directed its exact placement on the Madonna's chest. Then
the woman placed a white lace handkerchief in the statue's
hands. I saw that it was embroidered with a sentimental
"M"; the *portatore* said that the Madonna would use it to
"wipe away her tears." The handkerchief was a detail I had
not noticed before.

I thought of a photograph I had at home of Carolina,
taken just before she had immigrated to America in 1922.
Seated in a photographer's studio in Rome, she had posed
regally, although she was wearing the hairstyle and cotton
dress of a country woman. Her dark hair was pulled back
to reveal a handsome courageous face. My father "Romy,"
her youngest child at two, stood beside her in the chair,
and his siblings surrounded her. Aunt Amelia, the dutiful
daughter, was slightly behind; Uncle Gino, in front, wore
a sailor suit complete with a jaunty beret that was almost

a duplicate of the hats worn by the men in Trapani's procession. In this picture, Carolina looked like an immigrant Madonna, surrounded by her *portatori*. And her large, calloused hands clutched a handkerchief.

Perhaps it had been fashionable for women to carry handkerchiefs then, or perhaps they used them to keep the children clean, but I knew that Carolina had also had some tears to dry away. She had not wanted to go to America when the adventuring Antonio, already arrived in New Jersey, had sent her passage. In leaving Italy, she had also left her much-loved mother. For years Carolina had thought they would return; she had faithfully sent money back to an Italian bank, but during the Fascist regime it had disappeared. I remembered her crying when she came to visit us in Oregon: it had been forty years since Carolina had left Italy, and still they hadn't returned. Would she ever see her mother again? I couldn't imagine this pain, since I was so close to my own mother. And I wondered how my sons would feel if they were cut off from me in this way.

Here, in the Church of the Purgatory, the object of this Madonna's sorrow was several yards away on another platform. The statue of Christ stumbled under a cross while an exquisitely modeled Veronica, the woman who had helped him on the way to Calvary, held out a cloth. This was the *Ceto del Popolo*, the statue group belonging to "the people." It was the biggest platform, and twenty or more porters were needed to carry it. Carlo climbed onto this platform and put a silver necklace around Christ's neck, then replaced the wooden cross with one of solid silver. At Christ's feet, local florists stuck hundreds of tiny roses into the Styrofoam that covered the statue's base.

As I looked up at this apparition, the story of Demeter and Persephone came alive, as it had in Marsala. Was it Christ's flowing, feminine robes, which billowed out underneath the cross, that reminded me of Persephone? His silver jewelry, his fine-featured face? The bed of flowers he stood upon, as Persephone had on Lake Pergusa's shore? I glanced over at the Demeter-Madonna in her sweeping black cape as the porter jumped off the *ceto* and came over to me. He looked poignantly back at her. "You know," he said, "the *processione* is not really the story of Christ's death. It is about his mother, Mary, and the terrible thing he did to her by dying. Some people even think that Christ was irresponsible to get himself crucified like that. He was a miracle worker—why didn't he save himself and his mother from such sorrow?"

I walked around the other eighteen statue groups crowding the church. Each of these would be carried by twelve to sixteen *portatori* representing different Trapani trade guilds. In the corner was the *ceto* that would head the procession, "The Separation," with statues of Christ and Mary bidding each other farewell. Other *ceti* depicted Christ being crowned with thorns or hanging from his cross. Then there was the Pietà, carried by the members of the salt workers' guild, followed by the next-to-last *ceto*, a horizontal casket with the dead Christ inside. Last was the Madonna. Like Demeter, she would be alone in her search.

It was a predominantly male event, this decorating. The whole procession was really a man's event, including the revelry that had gone on every night since we had arrived in Trapani. Several times my family and I had joined Carlo and other *portatori* at a restaurant around the corner from our pensione for raucous three-hour dinners. I had been the only woman there in a sea of men; though I knew that being the *americana* was what kept me from being excluded, I was nonetheless pleased. And even I could not have been out like this without male chaperons.

These Sicilian dinners had provided a glimpse of Italian family life, albeit without the mothers. Antipasto, local peach-colored wine, mounds of spaghetti downed with more wine, and after-dinner liqueurs were voraciously consumed. Invariably, the joviality led to our singing the intermezzo from Mascagni's Sicilian opera, *Cavalleria Rusticana*, a tragic story of love, adultery, and death in a village near Palermo during Easter. Sometimes the *portatori* would sing the procession's songs. Once, we'd all donned funny hats that had decorated the restaurant's wall and had danced a zesty tarantella on the tabletops.

If Carolina could have seen me now! It saddened me to think of how, when she and Antonio had visited us in Oregon, she had spent her whole time cooking—just as Dina, the restaurant's cook, was now—creating similar Italian dinners when I was growing up. Dad had presided over repasts of chicken cacciatore or wild fish and game that he had caught. I loved those meals; there was something primal in our feasting. Carolina bustled about as those of us at the table all talked at once. Then, Dad would become the evening's storyteller: a comedy about Carolina easily shouldering a hundred-pound sack of chicken feed to Antonio's fifty-pound sack or about the "rocks" they had eaten as children in New Jersey because they were so poor. While everyone laughed, Carolina rarely left her kitchen post to sit down. Ever since, I had had an aversion to this "woman's work"; I didn't always provide my own family with fantastic, homemade meals. But I still hungered for the food and stories, and often, with my family, I would drop by my parents' house ten miles away to eat and recapture the past.

The men around me at these dinners were storytellers, too, talking into the night. Though many were single and didn't have wives or children at home, I couldn't understand how they could keep these late hours yet still manage to get to their work the next day. And though women were absent from these dinners, the men's stories were about them . . . especially about their mothers.

After the *Misteri* had been decorated, I joined the *portatori* with Tom, who had returned from Palermo, for a

"Last Supper" of sorts. Carlo and his friends were unusually thoughtful and focused on the procession to take place the next day, Good Friday. For many of them, it would be their tenth or even twentieth year of carrying, sometimes following a family tradition going back generations. What, I asked them, were they thinking when they shouldered their huge, one-ton weights?

Eagerly, Carlo answered, "We help Christ with his cross. Like Simon of Cyrene. Do you know the story?"

I nodded.

Carlo thought for a moment as if reliving other processions.

"But the big moment is when we return our *ceto* to the church on Saturday and when the Madonna comes in alone. We think of our mothers. The Madonna is our mother, too. At this moment we cry—for her, for all the mothers in the world."

Giuseppe, sitting quietly at Carlo's side, picked up his train of thought. He was a *cònsole*, or organizer, for the *Ceto Ecce Homo*, which depicted Pontius Pilate presenting Christ to the people. Now he began to hum one of the procession's songs. It was called *"Povero Fiore"* ("Poor Flower"), a sad, melodic tune whose title referred to the Madonna and her untimely loss.

Then the evening's surprise occurred. Giuseppe stood up, looking like an elf. He was a small man, shorter than me. He announced in Italian that the *Ceto Ecce Homo* needed a young boy to march in the procession and carry a pillow with medallions on it. He wanted Sky, now asleep back at the pensione, to do it.

"But it must be a surprise to him," Giuseppe cautioned, his mischievous eyes twinkling. "I will tell him tomorrow myself." With no children of his own, Giuseppe had taken a special liking to our boys. "Then we must find a blue suit and a bow tie," he continued. "And black dress shoes would be nice."

One seldom heard of outsiders participating in the procession. I remembered how, during the first procession, Tom had been asked to carry one of the platforms for a while. He had been proud to participate, even if only for an hour. But Giuseppe's invitation to Sky was different—it would be an honor to walk in the procession from start to finish. My head spun; I looked over at Tom and wondered how we would purchase the necessary items before the procession began. To complicate things, my mother, Gail Caperna, who was joining us for Holy Week, was arriving by train and ferry from Rome the next morning. The dinner ended a little earlier than usual; we all realized, a bit nervously, that there was much to do.

In the morning, Giuseppe arrived at the pensione with the news for Sky, who beamed as a maturing boy does upon being asked to join the ranks of older men. We walked to some shops, and I soon became a doting Sicilian mother, buying "grown-up" black dress shoes and even considering a $200 suit in a men's store. But Pina, the *signora* of our pensione, saved the day when I returned to think over the expensive purchase: her son, Mario, had outgrown the suit he had worn for Trapani's Mardi Gras the year before. Complete with eagle epaulets, it fit Sky perfectly. Tom and Mother arrived from the train station, just in time for her to do some quick hemming; then Sky dressed and was off to the barbershop with Giuseppe for a haircut.

At noon, I walked down to the church alone. The crowd gathering outside encircled a cordoned-off ramp that had been built overnight; inside, the church overflowed with hundreds of *portatori* placing last-minute decorations on the *Misteri*. I picked my way through the dark church, around the porters and other statues, to the Madonna, now moved to the back.

She seemed anxious to begin her search as the busy men below her darted about with flowers, candles, and

banners. Her black form rose up from the platform, covered with virtually every kind of Sicilian flower. It was
breathtaking. There were even hothouse poppies, the
flower that Persephone had picked at Pergusa.

I found Sky waiting with Giuseppe and his team as they
gathered around their *ceto*. In his new suit and with a stylish Italian haircut, Sky looked amazingly grown-up. I
wanted to talk with him, to go with him on this journey.

But I felt ignored and in the way. The *portatori* practiced
lifting the platform, top-heavy with its statues, while
Giuseppe, with his arm around Sky, was being inter-
viewed by a television crew from Palermo. Slipping quietly
out the church doors, I smiled at a large group of middle-
aged and old women at the bottom of the ramp, dressed in
black veils and coats. They were a women's confraternity
whom I had seen in the procession before; they would follow the Madonna's *ceto*. But because of their placement at
the end of the procession, they didn't seem to be a real part
of it. We chatted, and the women explained that they were
grieving with the Madonna because they had lost husbands, parents, or children to death. They looked almost
frightening with their ominous clothes and serious expressions.

Could I join them? I wondered.

They had pictures of the Madonna pinned to their
chests, which reminded me of Carolina, who always wore
scapulars and blessed medals around her neck. She would
have been at home with these women. One of them told
me, in a quiet and shaking voice, of her mother's death two
months before. In 1957, Carolina's own mother had died in
Italy. The two had never been reunited. From then on,
Carolina's eyes had held sadness that I often saw. It was
also then that she had found her only friend in the Blessed
Virgin and had begun to spend hours praying to her. Carolina had been wounded like these women in black. Help-

Trapani's women wear the Madonna's image like a scapular, close to their hearts; Procession of the Mysteries.

less in their grief, they trusted that the Madonna would understand their pain.

Did I have someone I wanted to grieve for? Would I fit into this women's group? If I did join, I would have to run back to the pensione and ask Pina if I could borrow a black dress. It all seemed so crazy. In any event, my halting Italian failed me as the women grew silent, staring at the closed church doors. I suddenly panicked, feeling the presence of death about me, and fled up some stairs to a nearby empty balcony.

Slowly the piazza in front of the church filled. The carabinieri had the hopeless task of keeping the crowd behind rope barricades. Twenty brass bands lined up at the church's side door as mothers ushered in their offspring, costumed as angels or brides of Christ, to join the procession. We all waited, watching the closed church doors. Then at exactly 3:00 P.M., the moment Christ had died, the doors rattled from inside and were thrust open. A cònsole in sunglasses stepped out and looked over the crowd. He gave a signal, and the Procession of the Mysteries began.

It took a full three hours for the church to empty. First to appear were forty eerie, white-hooded members of the Confraternity of Saint Michael; they walked out silently, their hooded robes recalling the sanbenito worn by pagans persecuted during the Spanish Inquisition. As with the masked actors I had seen in Marsala, their hidden faces signified the inner journey that together the Trapanesi would now make.

Then the music began. A brass band playing "Perdute Speranze" ("Lost Hopes") followed the hooded men. Next came a group of children dressed as Madonnas and little Veronicas holding cloths; then another confraternity, this time in purple hoods and black tunics.

The women in black, now watching solemnly to the left of the doors, crossed themselves as the portatori, struggling with short footsteps under the weight of the first ceto, "The

Separation," appeared. The platform barely fit through the doors; once out and down the ramp, the men slowly turned it to face a side street. Excited officials pushed the crowd out of the way. The band resounded with Grieg's "Funeral March" as, their feet in perfect unison, the carriers began the traditional waltz steps of the *annacata*. With utter grace and balance, they danced the immense *ceto* out of the square.

Cut off from the procession and the townspeople, I felt my own "separation" up on the balcony. I nervously scanned each statue group as it came out, looking for Sky. Finally, with the eighth group, I saw Giuseppe guiding the *Ceto Ecce Homo* out of the church. His men were bent over under the tremendous weight. Following close behind was a group of young girls, dressed in black and looking like miniature old women; in the center of them, proudly carrying his pillow, was Sky.

I waved from up above, but he didn't see me as he walked steadily down the ramp. He looked so Sicilian; I doubted if the crowd would know that he was a foreigner. The *Ceto Ecce Homo* made its way onto the street as the band played a doleful tune.

Now it was I who was the Madonna, watching my son leave me in this initiation rite he had been invited to join. I felt like Demeter watching Persephone disappear. But like the goddess and the Madonna, I realized I had to let him go. The procession was offering him a step toward independence from me.

Soon afterward, the *Ceto del Popolo* came through the doors. The platform was ablaze with flaming candles. Carlo caught sight of me above him and nodded, waving with his eyes, as he strained and grimaced under the weight of the statue.

Finally the mourning Madonna appeared in the doorway. Resplendent with flowers, she had never looked finer. The *portatori*, in bright red tunics and white surplices, reverently brought her down the ramp. Pinned to her skirt were countless offerings: photographs of children or notes asking for cures or favors. In the piazza, the men briefly set her down in order to fasten a canopy over her head. The mourning women in black fell in behind her; with the candles of her *ceto* sputtering, she was now ready to begin her eleventh-hour quest. Would she find her son? This, several Trapanesi had told me, was the age-old "mystery" that the procession was all about.

I climbed down from the balcony to follow the procession. At first I was at the end, with the women in black. Then I ran ahead, sometimes stopping to watch a *ceto* pass or moving to see another one approach. The procession was now a great undulating serpent, snaking its way through Trapani's labyrinthine streets. I waited, falling in to walk with the Madonna again. She moved slowly, stopping randomly at people's homes, hoping to find her son. Tearful mothers threw rose petals from their windows or brought sick children out to greet her. Others hung over balconies to let down baskets full of money offerings, which the *cònsole* emptied into metal collection boxes. Postcards of the Madonna were then placed in the baskets, and the donor would pull them up again.

I trailed along for several hours. The owner of a trattoria came out and suggested I walk up to his store's third-floor balcony. There I had a bird's-eye view of the procession as it entered the street. It had been moving in spurts; every block or so a *cònsole* would snap a wooden clacker called a *cioccola*, signaling for the porters to rest.

Below me, a *ceto* was set down with a great thud.

"*Volete un panino? Vino o caffè?*" asked the *cònsole.*

"*Sì!*" shouted the *portatori.* "*Tutto!*"

The *cònsole* popped into the trattoria and soon returned with sandwiches, bottles of wine, and plastic cups filled with coffee. With arms entwined around each other and the poles of the platform, the men ate and drank jovially.

Sicilian girls emulate the Madonna as they play the role of L'Addolorata *(the Sorrowing Mother); Procession of the Mysteries, Trapani.*

When they had finished, their cigarette smoke soon wafted up into the eyes of Saint John on the platform above them. The *cònsole* consulted his watch and snapped his *cioccola*. With cigarettes dangling from their lips, the men assembled quickly, and then the *ceto* was off again.

It was growing dark, and I hadn't found Sky and his *ceto*. The procession was slowly heading into New Trapani and would stop to rest on its broad boulevard. Some of the children would go home to sleep, rejoining the procession in the morning. Working my way through the crowd jamming the narrow street, I finally found Carlo's team; the *Ceto Ecce Homo* would be three ahead of them. I pushed on, and at last I spotted Sky. He was marching valiantly along. He almost didn't recognize me; then he seemed annoyed at my appearance. I asked how he was doing.

"My feet hurt," he said, finally succumbing to my mothering and pointing to his too-tight shoes. "But I'll be all right," he added. I estimated he had walked about four miles by now.

"Do you want to go on?" I asked.

He looked at Giuseppe, walking just ahead, who signaled for the *ceto* to stop. Giuseppe came over to greet me, beaming with joy. "Sky is *un bravo regazzo*," he said, "a good boy." He patted Sky's head affectionately, then reassured me, "I will see that he has something to eat when we rest on the boulevard."

Between Giuseppe and the girls dressed as old women, who were now surrounding us and listening attentively, my motherly role had been usurped.

"Yes," Sky answered firmly. "I will stay with the group and see you later tonight."

Giuseppe thumped on the poles of the platform with the *cioccola*. Like some Atlantean apparition, it rose and crept away through the candle smoke. Sky turned to me with a half-smile, then disappeared into the dark.

Now in the black night the procession became a frightening spectacle. With torches glowing, hooded confraternities came by like members of some Inquisitional auto-da-fé. Plaintive brass notes played a counterpoint to the drums' relentless bum-bum-ba-dum, as the *portatori*, arms and shoulders encrusted with wax from dripping candles and eyes glazed with exhaustion, continued on. Yet the carriers still waltzed the *annacata*, making the platforms sway like ships on a stormy sea. Watching in wonder as their legs intertwined, I thought of what the Greek writer, Lucian, had written: "The old mysteries were never performed without a dance."

I walked back once again to the procession's end to see the Madonna, now standing at the end of the boulevard. She had obviously not found her son; little did she know that he was on the *ceto* just ahead, already dead and lying in his coffin. The mourning women still surrounded her, their half-burned candles lighting up their tired faces. It was midnight, the journey's darkest hour. But theirs was not a solitary quest; they had each other. I, on the other hand, felt out of place and realized how few women were on the streets now, save for these women in black. From the strange stares I received from people in the crowd, I realized that I needed an escort. It was too dark, too late, for a woman to be out alone.

I worked my way back along the boulevard to the trattoria where I had agreed to meet Tom. We hadn't seen each other the whole day, and when I spotted him at a table in the back, he looked as exhausted as some of the carriers outside. His dark hair was matted, and his blue eyes were bloodshot.

"Can you guess what happened?" he asked, rubbing his shoulder and grimacing.

"No, what?"

"Carlo and the guys of the *Ceto del Popolo* asked me to be their *bilancino*. So I helped them carry for about three hours."

The hooded men in the Procession of the Mysteries harken back to secret confraternities during the Middle Ages; their garb is reminiscent of the sanbenito that pagan worshipers were forced to wear during the Inquisition.

"You're kidding!"

"Swear to God . . ."

I was impressed. It was one thing to be a *portatore* but quite another to be a *bilancino*. This was a job for someone tall and strong; it was strenuous because this person, by balancing the platform in front, carried more weight than any of the other men. And the *Ceto del Popolo*, the procession's largest statue group, weighed well over a ton. I knew that Tom's joining the procession a second time had given him, ironically, a kind of spiritual connection that he hadn't even come to Sicily to find. I laughed at the thought of how he had actually wanted to go on alone to Tunisia: how disappointed he had been when we had arrived too late for him to take the weekly ferry from Trapani!

"Where are Mother and Shane?" I asked, examining the bruises on his shoulder.

"Back at the pensione. How's Sky?"

Suddenly I felt a little envious. Both my son and Tom had been asked to join the procession, but I was still an observer . . . and an uninvited one at that, now that night had fallen.

"He wanted to keep going. But he looks pretty tired to me. I think we should find him and bring him back."

An hour later we found Sky, walking at the end of the boulevard. Limping, he seemed half-asleep; his eyes, meeting ours, took a while to focus. Many of the other children who had been walking with the *ceto* had already gone home.

"Let's go back to the pensione," I pleaded. "I'll wake you up at dawn and bring you back." Now he went willingly. Tom and I half-carried him through the thinning crowds back to our pensione. We walked down the darkened Corso Vittorio Emmanuelle, Old Town's main street; below the pensione, several people lingered, waiting for the procession's return in a few hours. Up in our room with

Mother and Shane next door, we put Sky—still dressed in his suit—in bed with us, and he fell asleep immediately.

"Clack-CLACK! Clackety-CLACK!" The sound of a snapping *cioccola* was only blocks away. I looked at the clock: it was 5:00 A.M. I woke Sky; Tom stayed behind as we grabbed our things and hurried down to the street. We walked two blocks past the Corso and saw the procession turn a corner. Women in chenille bathrobes looked down from their balconies. Old men peered out from the doorways of bars that had stayed open all night; others sat on chairs, nursing beers or coffee. We ran up and down the streets, looking for the *Ceto Ecce Homo*. Mothers with sleepy children hurried by in the gray light, and band members who had grabbed a few hours' rest picked up their instruments and ran to find the *ceto* they had left. Finally, along one of the crooked streets next to the boat harbor, we found Sky's team of carriers. Giuseppe was elated to see us.

The *ceto*'s band began warming up as Sky took his place among the girls. At any moment, said Giuseppe, the procession would begin its slow return to the church. "You see, the Madonna still hasn't found her son," he said wistfully. "Her last hope is that he will be inside the church."

I threaded my way back to the pensione, knowing that its position over the Corso would provide a good view of the procession as it passed below. I arrived to find Mother, Tom, and Shane surrounded by a crowd of fellow boarders on our balcony. Pina passed out strong cups of espresso. Joining them, I stood against the wrought-iron railing and watched as dawn lit the sky. In the pink glow, the shining white Moorish domes and arches around me came alive. One almost expected to hear the muezzin's call. Holy Saturday had come, and now Trapani's sons would bring their Great Mother home.

It took five hours for the Mysteries to inch down the Corso. I had forgotten that the music was so mournful and the early-morning light so melancholy, as the statues appeared through clouds of mist and smoke. Masses of people clung to each platform, helping the *portatori* dance with their loads. At last I saw Sky's lone figure, coming through the haze. He held his head high, keeping step with the band's rhythm. He, too, was waltzing. The people followed him excitedly, an occasional "Bravo!" surging up. Now everyone knew who he was. How honored the Trapanesi were that he had joined in and would now complete their sacred procession. I watched in amazement. He had always been timid about being onstage or before a large group in school, but now he was the epitome of self-confidence. Carlo and the carriers of the *Ceto del Popolo* came soon after the *Ceto Ecce Homo*. Carlo, now acting as the *bilancino*, spotted us on the balcony and smiled painfully. At least forty men hung onto the platform as if it were a lifeboat; many, I could see, had begun to cry.

The Madonna came last, lifelike as she bobbed along. Hundreds of people crowded around her. Captivated by the view below me, I forgot the time. Suddenly, Pina grabbed me. "I think you better go quickly!" she urged. "The *Misteri* will soon reach the church!" I ran down to the street and hurried to the piazza. It was overflowing with people. With the help of a police officer, I pushed my way through the crowd to the church doors.

What I had not counted on were my tears. As the dirge of the bands reached a crashing crescendo and I watched the *portatori* bring the *Misteri* home, I cried with them at the relinquishing of their load. When the *Ceto Ecce Homo* arrived, the men brought it up the ramp, paused, then set it down. They did not want to bring it inside, nor did they want the procession and their twenty-four hours together to end. Clutching each other in tears, they expressed a collective sorrow intermixed with joy. The men went in and out of the door three or four times, to the dismay of church officials who thought this dramatic "penetration" a bit too pagan. It was a sensual love act. They were entering the womb: mother, home, the church. Was it the mother to whom Persephone, after being trapped with Pluto, had returned? Or the woman whom Carolina had finally rejoined on her deathbed? Aunt Amelia had been the only one present when my grandmother had died in 1975. According to her, Carolina's last words, as if she had seen an apparition, were "Mother! I'm coming!" A look of longing had passed over her face. Then she had clutched Amelia's hand and died.

To the crowd's wild cheers, the still-waltzing *portatori* brought the platform through the doors one last time. As they came by, they were so close I could touch them. The final notes of the band, following close behind, echoed majestically from within the church. In climax, the carriers set the platform down with a loud thump, then sobbed in each others' arms. The only sounds now were their cries. Through my own tears, I had barely noticed Sky's entrance. He was too young to weep; instead, he smiled with pride at his journey's end.

Tom had hurried to join us, and together with Sky, we watched the remaining *portatori* and *ceti* come in, especially Carlo and the *Ceto del Popolo*. To the crowd's resounding roar, fifty men now guided it through the doors. An hour later, the last statues arrived: the Pietà, followed by the coffin with the dead Christ. All that remained was the Madonna.

At last she rounded the corner and stood in front of the church. The crowd grew silent, sensing her apprehension. Giuseppe, his eyes still moist, came over to us. He looked out admiringly at the Madonna. "Now she is afraid," he whispered. "Should she go into the church to look for Christ? If she does, she knows she must stay there—until next Easter!"

The distraught Madonna took nearly an hour to make up her mind, as up and down the ramp she went.

"Last year she went in very quickly," said Giuseppe. He shook his head. "I think this is a difficult year for her."

Finally, bidding the crowd farewell as flower petals showered down from balconies, the sadly swaying Madonna danced up the ramp and through the doors, entering the church. Her upright form, contrasted with the horizontal, dead Christ just before her, seemed a primal fertility symbol. It was a meeting of opposites: male and female, death and life. Yet even with all her dark power, the Madonna had to go on into the unknown. With the Trapanesi, I hoped she would find what she was looking for inside. Like Demeter and Persephone, or even Carolina, she had glimpsed Hades. She had looked death in the face. But unlike my grandmother, she had not been defeated by death. She seemed to have come through it alive.

Once the Madonna was inside, the doors were immediately banged shut. With tears barely dried, the job of dismantling began, as carriers, band members, and friends removed flowers and candles from the platforms. They took the silver swords from Pontius Pilate's soldiers; one unfastened the Madonna's silver heart, which had been pinned to her breast, and placed it in a box. A man walked by with a statue of Christ, which had been in Mary's lap on the *ceto* of the Pietà, cradled in his arms like a baby. There was mad commotion everywhere, and Tom and Sky had disappeared in the crowd to look for Carlo and Giuseppe. I talked awhile with some *portatori* and townspeople who milled about; like me, they did not want to leave. I walked around, red-eyed and aimless, until a young boy came up and tugged on my arm. "*Signorina*, I know a place where you can take a beautiful photograph. Follow me!" he insisted. I could see that he was motioning to the choir loft above us.

I followed, thinking that he was right; it would offer a good vantage point. We made the long climb up a narrow and unstable stairway behind a door in a corner of the

church. Finally we were in the loft, high above the sanctuary. But before I had a chance to evaluate the view, this
Sicilian boy, who wasn't much older than Sky, grabbed me
and tried to kiss me on the lips. I was shocked. In my best
but nervous Italian, I shouted, "*Per favore, ragazzo, per favore. No!*" I fled down the stairway, with him clamoring after. I felt I was in a Fellini film. I had heard about these
"experienced" Sicilian boys. When I made it back to the
church floor, I found the room practically empty, save for
the skeletal-looking *Misteri* now back in their positions;
Sky, Tom, and all the *portatori* had left. In a procession
where I had had difficulty finding my place, I had been denied the denouement by a thrill-seeking boy. Yet, I mused,
how quickly he had reminded me that life and resurrection
do follow winter and death!

I waded through the debris and passed the now-silent
Madonna. What had she found in the church? Where was
her son? It *was* a mystery. If she had found Christ, as Demeter had found Persephone, I knew that she would lose
him again and again every year, just as winter would follow spring and summer. It seemed so painful. But most important, with the Madonna the journey had been made.
With her help, the whole town had entered the unknown
together.

I felt my own journey had just begun. I knew that I had
to find the meaning of the dark Madonna's power, the
power that Carolina and so many women had lost or
relinquished—or had never had. As a woman, it often
eluded me, too, and I was acutely aware of this here in Sicily. Yet, I wondered, could the women of Sicily help me
. . . if I could get to them? Perhaps I would find this
power if I journeyed back to the places where the old deities like Demeter had once lived.

I wanted to join the family of Sicilians I had found in
Trapani—but on my own terms. Tom and Sky, as males,
had gained entrance so easily. Still, I knew that with Sky's

initiation into the procession, I had been partially freed. A bit of the old me had been left behind, the me that was like Carolina: only—and always—a mother.

I glanced back at the Madonna one last time; as Giuseppe reminded me, she would wait in the dark church another year before coming out to search again. I felt as alone as she, as afraid as Demeter watching Persephone disappear. I said good-bye and opened the church doors, startled by the brilliant sunlit afternoon. For now, spring had come again.

CHAPTER II

The Levanzo Cave

WITH THE PROCESSION OVER, we all planned to spend another week in Sicily, making side trips from Trapani. I was the first one up on Easter Sunday; this was the official day of the resurrection, but I didn't feel particularly jubilant. Although I had more or less caught up on my sleep the night before, I still felt drained from the intense emotions of the procession. It was a letdown now, with the town unbearably quiet in comparison to Friday and Saturday. No one was outside; it seemed the Trapanesi were preoccupied with celebrating Easter in the confines of their homes.

While everyone slept in, I stole down to the Corso for a cappuccino, then set out for a walk. I passed the cathedral and its clanging bells that were announcing Easter; plump matrons, dressed in expensive and stylish outfits, stood chatting on the church steps. Their husbands, looking like characters from a *Godfather* film, doted on equally well-dressed children, showed solicitude for their wives, and greeted passersby. It was such a picture of family togetherness. But I felt oddly irritated.

I remembered scenes from my own childhood. Sunday mass for our family had been a time of similar solidarity. We kids would get dressed up, Mom and Dad short of temper because we were late for church. We would hurry off, someone invariably crying in the backseat. Afterward, we would go to Sambo's Restaurant where Dad would show off his smartly clad daughters and handsome young son. But I disliked Sundays, then and now. I didn't like to put on a pretense of decorum; I preferred the disorganization and casualness of the rest of the week: dressing in jeans, taking part in rambunctious neighborhood baseball games, creating messy art projects in the garage. Dad usually arrived home late from work, and we kids would sneak out of bed to greet him. Sometimes we didn't see him on school nights, and having eaten alone with Mother, we would wait for the next Sunday when we could be together again.

These Sicilian families were partly like that. The reality was that most of the time, women took care of the domestic chores while the men escaped whenever they could, chatting on the streets with their friends or playing cards in the bars. But they always returned home to eat, which is where these parading families were going now. Eating kept the family together: *"La famiglia sempre . . . A mangiare!"* ("The family always . . . Let's eat!")

The thing that made our family different was my mother's ongoing struggle for independence from a tradition-minded Italian husband. By now, they had reached a tenuous compromise: Dad was probably on a fishing trip back in the States; Mother, upstairs in the pensione, was only vaguely wondering what he was doing. Finding other things to fill her life, she had relinquished the idea of an Ozzie and Harriet marriage and of children who would lead "normal" lives. We were raised a somewhat rebellious bunch. I preferred to call us adventurous, and Mother was, too. She was a creative and conscientious wife and mother, but perhaps because she was an artist and had undertaken a college education when in her fifties—not to mention the stubborn streak she had inherited from her Swiss-German ancestors—she had sought and found a bigger world, beyond the humdrum of domestic life, to explore. And she had opened this world up to us kids. When I was a teenager, every summer she had packed my sisters, brother, and me into our family jeep, hitched a trailer to the back, and taken us on a monthlong camping trip through the western states. Dad didn't like this trailer travel, but she had been content to go alone. She brought books along, and we would study Indian and cowboy lore as we visited gold-mining towns in Colorado or remote Pueblo Indian ruins in New Mexico. A nature expert, she taught us about everything from bunchgrass to Indian healing herbs. She liked being on the road alone and the sometimes dangerous situations that arose; I remember her excitement as she followed a Navajo guide in the jeep, fording an arroyo where the water came up to the door frames in order to reach the Canyon de Chelly cliff dwellings in Arizona. I was amazed by her fearlessness of grizzly bears when we camped in Glacier National Park, and once, she had walked miles for help when the jeep broke down on a deserted Nevada highway.

Now that I was older, our roles were a bit reversed: Mother was eager to join me on my various travels, and I always invited her along. This time she had arrived in Sicily with a backpack, ready for anything.

When I returned to the pensione, I found everyone awake. We discussed our plans for the coming week, and I suggested we begin with a hike across Levanzo, a small island ten miles off the Trapani coast and part of the Egadi island chain.

I knew there was a cave on this island; called the Grotto Genovese, it was reachable by a three-mile goat trail. Inside the cave, which was seldom seen by tourists, were pictographs dating from 10,000 B.C., one of the oldest records of Sicily's Paleolithic history. I had been intrigued by a pamphlet from the Trapani tourist office, for it said that among the paintings was an image of a woman called *la dea*, or the "goddess of the grotto." I wondered who she was. Was it possible that she bore some distant relationship to the ancient goddesses that I sought?

We decided not to go the next day, since it was Easter Monday, an Italian holiday, and bookings would be impossible on the local ferries. But with a picnic lunch of Sicilian bread, salami, cheese, and wine stuffed into our day packs, we set off on Tuesday.

Carlo, having reluctantly agreed to come along, met us at the ferry landing. He was hung over from partying with his *portatori* friends the night before. Looking terrible, he was unenthusiastic about our trek; American-style hikes were foreign to him. He had barely heard of the cave and thought the whole idea was a waste of time.

"Why look for a stupid cave?" he asked as we headed up the gangplank.

"It's not just a cave. Inside are the oldest paintings in all of Sicily," I said defensively.

"But why do you like all these old things?" He seemed genuinely perplexed. He looked out across the harbor, admiring the modern skyline of Trapani's New Town, where he lived. "It is better that Sicily forget the past."

"But doesn't understanding the past help us to understand the present? Or the future?" I asked.

"I don't know." He shook his head. "I think you're crazy."

Sicilians have never understood a Westerner's fascination with antiquities. Soccer matches are more to their liking than ancient caves or even than Sicily's renowned Greek temples, such as those at Segesta or Agrigento. Knowing this, I decided not to tell him now about the goddess of the cave.

View of Levanzo and Favignana islands from the Trapani coast.

Mother had studied Greek mythology. But to her, as to many of her generation and even mine, goddesses were floaty figures in Bulfinch's *Mythology* or Edith Hamilton's, who sat passively on thrones somewhere on Mount Olympus. Styled and interpreted by the patriarchy of Greece's Golden Age, these women appeared as wives or lovers of gods like Zeus or Adonis. They were like Grandmother's Virgin Mary: beautiful, no doubt, but they didn't do much. They watched the male gods create worlds or people; they had no major effect on culture. Would the goddess of the cave be different?

The ferry churned across the straits separating Trapani from Levanzo. Carlo took the boys to visit the pilothouse, and Mother sat inside reading her guidebook. Tom and I stood near the roped-off bow. I felt a sense of expectation, conscious of how much myth and history had passed through these waters around us.

Porpoises swam alongside the ferry, reminding me of those that had guided Ulysses through this "wine-dark" sea. He, too, had gone into the underworld, bid by the sirens and Circe. In fact, Samuel Butler, a nineteenth-century English scholar, believed that *The Odyssey* had taken place off the Trapani coast and had been authored by a wealthy Trapani woman in 1000 B.C., instead of by Homer. How was it, I wondered, that this noblewoman of "Drepanum" could have known so much about Ulysses' male journey? Perhaps she had gone herself. I mused over the possibilities.

Tom interrupted my thoughts as he shouted above the roar of the ferry's engines. "Weren't the Punic Wars fought somewhere around here?" he asked, looking southward.

"All through this channel here—and hundreds of other battles." I pointed across the sea toward Marsala, now imagining the Punic ships surging through these straits, prows carved with animal heads breasting in the waves. I pictured their foes, the Romans, with newly invented *corvi*, the amphibious ships that brought a sea battle onto land in the First Punic War in 241 B.C. Later, the Moorish corsairs had sought shelter in the Egadi Islands' hidden grottoes. In more recent times, Garibaldi with his thousand "Red-shirts" had passed through these straits to land at Marsala and defeat the Neapolitan Bourbon troops in 1860. Nor did I forget the Allies who, nearly a century later, had sped by in their landing craft to expel the Axis forces from Sicily at the end of World War II. Even Dad had been through here during the war; little did he know that I would return to look for ancient drawings in an obscure Levanzo cave.

"There it is. It looks pretty bleak," said Tom, pointing straight ahead.

The jagged outline of the island now appeared through the mist; light-colored, with no vegetation, it looked like a mirage.

The ferry slowed, then puttered into Levanzo's harbor; rosy beige-colored tufa cliffs towered above us. A few fishermen stood on the dock to greet the boat; otherwise, the island looked deserted.

"You should see it here in the summer," said Carlo, join-ing us with the boys as we all trooped down the gang-plank. He looked into the transparent water. "Hundreds of people come to swim in the sea. Now it is too cold." He zipped up his jacket disgustedly while I, energized by what was, for me, balmy weather, stripped down to a T-shirt. I jogged up the pathway, passing the deserted Villa Gioia, a wind-beaten eighteenth-century fortress that could have been a setting from Lampedusa's *The Leopard*. I was impa-tient, for I knew that the climb to the cave would be mostly uphill. We would also have to find a guide to unlock the cave's gate. I was worried, too, for I hoped to photograph the cave's paintings, and as was typical at many museums or archaeological sites in Sicily, no flash would be allowed.

We arrived at an empty café overlooking the seafront and ordered cappuccinos and sodas from a lone bartender

Conversation on the beach; Trapani coast.

who was busily scrubbing the counter. Soon a teenage boy appeared at the door. We asked him about the cave. When we arrived there, he said, a goatherd who lived nearby would unlock the gate.

"What about taking photographs?" I asked.

"Oh, no, that is never allowed," he said firmly.

I felt irritated with this Italian penchant for obeying the rules. Perhaps they were still recovering from the days of Mussolini or from centuries of living under their many conquerors. It never seemed to occur to them to try to get around the rules or to buy off the powers-that-be. I decided I would do just that, if I had to, and slung my camera bag over my shoulder. The boy eyed it disapprovingly as we hurried off in the direction he had pointed out, toward a road above the town.

Our hike soon became a stiff uphill climb; tall fennel, agave cactus, and prickly pear struggled out of the rocky landscape that fell away below us. The road turned into a goat path. Carlo lagged behind with Tom; Mother and I took the lead, while the children ran back and forth between the two contingents. We all seemed to be making this hike for different reasons. For Mother, it was a proving ground, a chance to test her physical abilities. For the children, it was an adventure to gaze at passing donkeys and their riders, race each other, or throw rocks down the ravines. Tom was along because he liked hiking and was curious about the island's landscape. Caves intrigued him, but he was skeptical about the goddess I hoped to find. Carlo was the reluctant male guide; he knew we might need his help if we encountered difficulty. But the hike to him seemed like a forced march.

I was on a pilgrimage; in some ways, I wished I were journeying alone. But though obsessed with what I would find in the cave, I was half-afraid of my compulsion to go down into these dark places. Cave exploration was a group activity for a reason, I suspected; for now, I was glad that my family was along.

We reached the highest point on the island, probably fifteen hundred feet above the sea. At the hill's crest, we could see all the Egadi Islands to the east, the direction from which we'd come. Ten thousand years ago, before the sea had cut its ten-mile swath, these rocky islands had been joined to Sicily's landmass. Some scholars proposed that the Egadi Islands had been the first arcade of a bridge uniting Europe to Africa, two hundred miles to the southwest across the Mediterranean.

We headed west down the mountain to Levanzo's windward side. The path petered out, and soon we were making our own way, pushing through the scrub. From a clearing, I looked down to the beach far below us; there I could see an immense tufa outcropping jutting into the sea. From the boy's description, this had to be the cave.

Ominous clouds moved in, warning us of rain. A flock of goats hurried up the slope, followed by a cane-waving boy. These islanders were more sensible than we were. They were heading toward the island's leeward side. The agave and dense scrub clogged the hillside; we had to feel our way gingerly. For another half hour, we stumbled toward the cave.

Then we were out of the scrub. Just below us was the tufa grotto towering a hundred feet in the air and surrounded by a crashing surf.

I wondered if the boy at the café had at his command some form of telepathic communication or the services of some Andean-like system of mountain runners. For at the base of the grotto stood the goatherd he had said would be there, a man of about forty. It had begun to rain a little, and his goats huddled nearby under a large agave. He seemed to be waiting for us.

"Are you the gatekeeper?" I asked, out of breath.

"*Sì, signora.* I can take you in. The entrance is over there."

He pointed to a three-foot-high grate covering a hole in the rock. We all walked over, with the man following.

"I would like to photograph the paintings inside," I stated firmly. "Is that possible?"

He frowned. "No. There will be only torchlight inside, and flash will harm the paintings."

I was upset, and Carlo intervened.

"*Signore,* she wants just one photo."

"No," insisted the man. He was not budging.

"I will not use flash," I promised. "*Per favore?*"

The man eyed my tripod, already in my hand. I hadn't mentioned money and was about to, when he relented. "Only one photo. And you must make it quickly. Come, we must go at once." He unlocked the gate and lit a torch. We crouched down and, one by one, entered the cave.

A musty, empty smell of stale air permeated the unused space. A passageway spiraled around, like a chambered nautilus, as we edged carefully through the tunnel. Behind me, the children and Tom shouted to hear their echoes, Carlo swore in Sicilian as he stumbled on a rock, and Mother chatted with the guide. I felt claustrophobic and remembered once when, as a child, I had been briefly lost in a cave in northern California. It had only been two or three minutes until my friends had heard my panicked cries, but I hadn't had a flashlight, and the darkness, so absolute, had felt like death. It was irrational, this fear of darkness and subterranean places.

Our descent, though, was brief. We came to a circular grotto. The passage had ended somewhere in the rock's center. The guide held his torch high and told us to look up to our right on the grotto's wall.

Black, childlike images of stick men and animals suddenly danced across the wall in the flickering torchlight. There were twenty or thirty of them, drawn boldly with carbon. Some images appeared to be in front of the others, placed higher or lower on the wall to show perspective. Some were incised, by stone tool, with great precision. It was a Paleolithic blackboard, as if a classroom of children had each contributed to this communal mural.

"You see, here is a deer," pointed out the guide with great solemnity. "And here," holding his torch higher, "is a bison. We do not know what all the animals are. Of course, there are many men. They are probably dancing."

Where was the female divinity I had come to see? I scanned the wall in frustration.

It was Mother who found her.

"Susan, is that the goddess?" She pointed excitedly to the edge of the wall.

Because she was so large, we almost hadn't seen her. A black form, she loomed among the dancing men and animals. With a small head, she was spade-shaped and pregnant-looking, like an inverted triangle. She looked like a stylized version of the terra-cottas I had seen of Persephone and Demeter, or even of the black-shrouded *Madonna Addolorata*. Another bulbous female shape nearby seemed to be holding onto a large bison with a rope.

"Do you know what this figure is?" I tested the guide, pointing to the larger image.

"I don't know . . . Perhaps a woman. It is hard to say."

Tom and the boys looked closely. Shane, who was the most interested, studied the form a moment and then proclaimed it to be Darth Vader.

I was sure the figure was a woman. "Could it be a female god?" I ventured to the guide.

"Maybe . . . But I think there is—what you call—*una dea* up here." He held the torch up to a niche on our far right, which he hadn't shown us yet.

Here was another large female figure, apparently seated on a throne. She was painted red, the Paleolithic color for menstrual blood and fertility. She was even bigger than the other female figures. I wondered why the guide hadn't pointed her out before.

Though she had been painted thousands of years before the Greeks appeared in Sicily, I imagined her as a distant forerunner of Persephone seated on her throne in Hades. And perhaps the other female figures were foremothers of Demeter, come to visit her newfound daughter.

Because of their shapes and sizes, these females dominated the cave. Yet they had joined with the male and animal figures. The men—or women—who had painted them had imbued them with a kind of mysterious knowledge; they seemed to promise fertility, with their bulbousness and red color. And although Paleolithic scholars usually thought that the male figures were hunters, I couldn't believe that this mural was about hunting. The men held no spears. They, the females, and the animals seemed to be celebrating life and rejuvenation in this dark grotto. They were joyous; as the guide had said, they were dancing.

What had happened to the world in the intervening twelve thousand years? Why was there now such a division between male and female? Now the female deity was seldom honored, except perhaps as the Virgin Mary. Yet until the time of Christ, the old goddesses had been powerful and active, suggesting that women then had been, too. Persephone had gone into Hades; before her, the Babylonian Inanna, goddess of love and harlots, had descended willingly into the underworld to meet her devouring sister, Ereshkigal.

But Carlo, still feeling obstinate, wanted to disallow the presence of females in the cave.

"To me, they look like kings dressed in robes," he said, scrutinizing the forms on the first wall, which the guide had lit again.

"I don't know . . . she could be right," conceded Tom.

"Darth Vader," repeated Shane.

The guide interrupted our deliberations. "*Signora*, you

must take your photo. We can only stay a few minutes more."

I had almost forgotten that I wanted a record of this cave, an icon to guide me on my journey. While Mother held my bag, I quickly set up the tripod and camera. Guessing at the time, I made a long exposure lit by the guide's torch.

My lens opened and shut; then our guide extinguished his torch and, as quickly as the mysterious paintings had been revealed to us, they disappeared. The guide led us out of the cave.

Outside, the storm clouds had passed, and Tom and I prepared a picnic on some craggy black rocks just down the beach from the cave. Mother and the boys threw rocks down into the surf as Carlo, now happy at the prospect of eating, stretched out in the sun and waited eagerly. It was not *la cena*, but the sandwiches would do. When lunch was ready, Tom commandeered a spot on one rock with Carlo and the boys, while Mother and I perched on another and watched the water below us. It was a beautiful spot, the dark tufa contrasting dramatically with the shimmering water.

Mother studied the grotto's entrance, then looked out to sea.

"How do you suppose they got here, the people who came to this cave?"

"No one knows for sure," I said. "Maybe from Africa on the land bridge. It's a mystery. Many archaeologists think they came by boat from Spain."

"Wherever they came from, do you think they brought the cave goddess with them?" Mother, ever supportive, was always interested in my theories.

"They could have. The caves in southern Spain have similar female forms." I thought of spade-shaped females I had seen in photographs from Paleolithic caves in Spain and of terra-cotta figures dating from 6000 B.C. at Catal Hüyük in Turkey.

Tom, who had come over for another sandwich, overheard us. "Remember those Anasazi pictographs we saw in the southwest United States? Where was it—Tres Piedras? Mesa Verde?"

He was right. Anasazi Indians, the Southwest's ancient cliff dwellers, had painted and carved similar forms on the rock walls of their pueblo-style dwellings. But the cradle of this Great Mother had probably been in the ancient Near East; from there, scholars thought the first migrations had brought her around the world.

We finished our lunch; Carlo took a nap while Tom and the boys explored the surreal formations made by some tufa outcroppings nearby. After a while, Carlo woke up and the boys and Tom returned. Everyone was tired and wanted to go. I gathered up our garbage—an empty wine bottle, papers, and Styrofoam cups—and stuffed them into a bag. It was a sizable collection, and Carlo, thinking himself gentlemanly, took the bag from me.

"You don't need to carry that. Here, we can just throw it away." And with a great heave, he threw it into the sea.

I was stunned.

"Carlo—you can't do that!" I looked out at the huge floating bag. It was too late to retrieve it, already swirling out in the foamy waves. Although for many Italians the sea was a limitless refuse dump, to me his action was an insult to this sacred place.

I stared angrily at Carlo. He was surprised at my reaction and, chagrined, loped meekly up the rocks. I myself darted up, though in a different direction, through the scrub.

Tom shortly caught up with me. "Leave him alone," he advised. "It's just a sack of garbage."

It did seem ridiculous, but I knew the real origin of my hostility was Carlo's inability to take my quest to this island seriously. Still annoyed, I charged up the hill ahead of everyone. Besides, it was late; now we had to worry about getting back in time to make the last ferry to Trapani.

As I got halfway up the hill, the terrain looked different; though I had laid a sight-line at the hill's bottom, we were soon struggling through much higher scrub than before. I couldn't see the crest of the hill, where we needed to come out, and the pitch was much steeper. I knew we had taken the wrong route, yet I stubbornly persisted. A few minutes later, the hill became so steep that I couldn't continue.

The others caught up, and we began to argue about which way to go. Tom, Mother, and I decided we needed to go more to the left; although I could tell that Carlo did not agree, he said nothing. We worked our way around a sharp ravine as, way behind us, Carlo headed the other direction. What was he doing?

"I've found it!" yelled Carlo, halfway back down the hill and some two hundred yards to the right. I could see his arms and head flailing among the scrub. I hurried down to him, recognizing landmarks from our descent to the cave. This was the path.

Before I could say anything, Carlo looked down. "I'm sorry I threw that sack into the sea," he said.

I felt ashamed of my anger and told him so.

Then he surprised me by saying, "And thank you for taking me to the cave."

We all walked back up the hill. At the crest I looked down for a last view of the grotto. The sea was now a deep azure, spectacular in the dying sun; a shadow fell, turning the grotto a reddish black. I made a last mental image of the deity hidden inside, then we quickly descended the hill to the waiting ferry.

It was good that I remembered her in this way. For when we got back to Trapani and I went to unload my camera, I found it empty. In my haste at the cave, I hadn't checked to see if it was loaded. I had made an exposure into an empty camera—into nothing. She was elusive; now I would have to work doubly hard to find her. I would have only her fleeting image in my head.

CHAPTER III

Journey to Enna

"I'LL SEE YOU TOMORROW. Be careful!" Mother waved, then stepped spryly onto the bus at Palermo's central station, where we had arrived earlier that day from Trapani. Immediately, she forgot about me and was chattering with the conductor in her rudimentary Italian. The bus eased into the heavy line of traffic on its way to the Teatro Massimo, where she was going to see a Pirandello play.

I envied her, realizing now how much freer she was to travel alone in Sicily than I. The problem wasn't one of encountering physical dangers but of breaking age-old sexual mores. Because older women were presumed to be less sexual than women of my age, it was more acceptable for women like Mother to be "out." I felt uncomfortable with the disapproving stares I received when traveling anywhere alone.

Nevertheless, I was now embarking on a bus trip to Enna, a history-rich hill town known as "Sicily's navel" because it is located at the island's exact center. Tom had decided not to come; the weather had warmed up, and he had taken the boys to a beach resort near Selinunte. But I wasn't without company; a professor friend from Oregon, Barbara Corrado Pope, was in Sicily during her spring break to do research and was meeting me that afternoon in Palermo. I had met Barbara when she headed the Women's Studies Program at the University of Oregon, where I had taught in 1987. Like me, Barbara was of Italian ancestry. Now she was headed for the archaeological museum in Syracuse, then directly back to Palermo. I planned to go with her as far as Enna, where we would visit the site where Sicily's greatest Greek temple to Demeter had once stood. I owed a lot of my inspiration to Barbara, for it was she who had first explained to me the Sicilian version of the myth of Demeter and Persephone.

I walked to Barbara's hotel, where she was waiting, dressed in a trench coat and holding a stack of photocopied articles brought from the States. We returned to the station and caught a bus. Settling in our seats, we began the slow ascent to Enna, a hundred miles inland from Palermo.

"I think I've got something for you," said Barbara, shuffling through the sheaf of papers. She handed me an article about the temple at Enna, showing the nearby Lombardy castle, which had been built during the Norman era and then restored by Frederick II in the fourteenth century.

"It says the Sicilians believe that Demeter is buried there, under the tower. With the Sicani king, Sicanus. Can you believe it?" She laughed. Barbara was more of a skeptic than I; after all, Demeter and Sicanus were supposed to be mythical. But secretly, I did want to believe it.

"Look at this," Barbara continued, rustling through the pages. She came to a poorly photocopied reproduction of an Enna church. "It says that on this church's altar, until the end of the last century, stood statues of Greek gods."

"What do you think?" I said, looking at the paper with interest.

"Who knows?" She laughed again. "But we should try to find the church."

It sounded intriguing: I knew the old religions had been integrated with Catholicism when Sicily became Christianized in the fourth century. And Enna was considered a bastion of folk tradition, even now. But the reality was that Christianity had been in Sicily for fifteen hundred years, interrupted only by the Moorish occupation. Actual pagan statues in a Catholic church seemed unlikely.

The highway from Palermo ran east toward Catania; it was a modern wonder built on concrete pillars soaring high over steep ravines and riverbeds. Our bus lumbered along, coughing diesel fumes, as vacationing Sicilians passed by, tooting the horns of their Fiats and Alfa Romeos. About fifty miles inland, we turned south and traversed the foothills of the Madonie Mountains, whose major peaks rose straight up, their tops obscured by a heavy mist. They were fortresslike, majestic. They reminded me of the sturdy museum terra-cottas of Demeter; their fallen boulders formed her breasts, and the creases in the rock outlined her stern, benevolent face. In the summer this was a harsh, desolate area, scorched and yellowed after the wheat harvest. Now, soft fields with green shoots trembled; the humans who had planted them were nowhere to be seen. Dusk was settling in. A few sheep clustered on the rocky hillsides as, from occasional stone houses, thin columns of smoke swirled up like a watercolor wash.

We began the upward climb to Enna. We couldn't see it, for it was perched so high that the mist blotted it out. After a series of dizzying switchbacks, the driver stopped at a pullout to check the engine; I got off for a moment to get some air. It was dark and cold, my light jacket useless in the mountain chill. We were obviously at a high altitude, but Enna still wasn't anywhere in sight.

The bus continued for another forty-five minutes; in contrast to the descent to Levanzo's grotto, we now climbed straight up as if heading right off the earth. Finally, we cut through the clouds and were on the very top of the mountain; ramparted walls appeared out of nowhere, and the lights of Enna twinkled above us.

We disembarked at a deserted bus station on the edge of town. It was late. Quickly, we headed up a narrow cobblestoned street toward a hotel that the bus driver had told us about, hoping there would be a vacancy. Dogs barked and an old woman, looking out her window, eyed us suspiciously. Behind her, inside the room, a votive light flickered in front of a statue of the Virgin.

A group of young men stood on the corner, joking and making indecipherable remarks in Sicilian as we passed by; they seemed convinced that we, as American tourists, were traveling without escorts in order to find love with someone just like them. These men were boyish versions of my father, with dark eyes and hair and, even in a remote place like Enna, designer clothes. They exuded self-confidence and vitality. Most Sicilian men had this passionate quality. They showed it in the way they talked excitedly in bars or in the way they walked, strutting. It was an exaggerated and self-absorbed passion, and it could be offensive or it could be moving, like the passion of the *portatori* in the procession, crying in each other's arms.

But I rarely saw the passion of the Sicilian women. Were they hiding it somewhere? What had they done with it? As with Carolina, had it gone into the spaghetti pot, the Virgin Mary, or into worry about their sons? I wondered if passion, for Sicilian women, existed at all.

Another old woman, tugging at a frayed shawl around her shoulders, peered at the men from her window just inches from the narrow street. She sighed, shutting the window and switching off the light.

Night had come to Enna.

It was a long walk up to the town's center. When we arrived, the desk clerk at the Hotel Enna was still up. A bare bulb burned above his head, casting green shadows on his face. He looked us over, then checked his ledger. An idle bellhop sat on a torn sofa, smoking a cigarette.

"That will be $30 apiece," the desk clerk informed us. The price was high for Sicily, but we took the room gratefully. He handed us a key. "But the elevator is not working. You will have to use the stairs." He showed us ceremoniously to the stairwell and bowed.

The bellhop accompanied us to the sixth floor and let us into the small room. Pink and white towels embroidered with "Hotel Enna" lay on the bed and sink, brightening the furnishings. We opened the drapes that covered the balcony door; stepping out, we realized we were overlooking the whole town. Tile rooftops arced below us, and a few lights from houses still glowed. Below hung the dense cloud cover through which the bus had climbed. We now seemed to be in another world.

In the morning, we dressed and descended to have a quick breakfast in the hotel's dining room. We walked immediately to the town's highest point, a rock outcropping a few blocks away with a 360-degree view of Sicily. Here, Demeter's great temple had once stood. I had imagined a few Ionic columns or at least a tumble of rocks. I was disappointed. Nothing remained on the outcropping except some worn slabs that had been the temple's base. Around them was a garish metal railing, an eyesore meant to keep sightseers from falling off the rock.

It was a long drop, about five hundred feet, to a wide, grassy shelf below. Beyond that, a mile farther down, was the valley from which we had come. Across it to the north was Calascibetta, another hill town five miles away. To the east it was just possible to see a faint outline of Mount Etna, Sicily's renowned active volcano. I stood on the rock imagining Demeter surveying her fields. How impressive her temple must have been. Now she would have been dismayed to see the fields below us crisscrossed with freeways running to Palermo and Catania.

Demeter enthroned; terra-cotta, 500 B.C., found at Locri, Italy; National Museum of Reggio Calabria.

And what of her daughter Persephone, picking wild-flowers on the shore of Lake Pergusa far below? I searched the distant valley and found the lake about two miles to the south, looking stagnant and surrounded by refineries spewing smoke. I had difficulty imagining Persephone there on its shores. A racetrack now traced the lake's circumference; in the annual summer tournaments, it seemed that sports cars had long since replaced the lusty Pluto on his chariot.

Just then a man sauntered over; he was about fifty and wore a tan corduroy jacket and a tweed cap set on his head at an angle. "The lake of Persephone . . . it is *bellissima*, like you two *signorine*. Can I take you there?"

I had noticed him watching us from his car; he had gaped when I ducked the railing and climbed out to the rock's very edge for a better view.

"No, thank you, *signore*," Barbara said firmly.

"But perhaps you can help us," I ventured. "We are looking for a church in Enna—where there were statues of Greek gods until only a hundred years ago."

"It's impossible," he said. "Only Christ and the saints are in the church."

"But look," I said. I pulled the photocopy out of my bag. "It says they were in this church . . . Do you know where it is?"

He stared at the paper. "That is the church by the main square," he announced. "But it is impossible. Statues of Christ, of Mary . . . of San Francesco, San Antonio, yes. But there are no pagan gods in the church."

He was indignant. We would not accompany him to the lake, and now we thought Greek gods were worshiped in Enna. We gathered up our things and thanked the man. He sauntered back to his car, then leaned against it, looking dejected. He watched us go, hoping that other *signorine* less strange than we would come, on this bright morning, to Demeter's rock.

We walked down the road to Piazza Marconi and found what appeared to be the church. It was closed, but a woman passing by said that it would open at 4:00 P.M. Barbara looked at her watch. It was 1:00 P.M., and in two hours her bus would leave for Syracuse. I would have to inspect the church on my own. We bought bread, olives, and cheese in a market, then went back to the square for picnic lunch. The piazza was deserted, save for a flock of pigeons. Right in front of us, in a defunct fountain, was a large bronze casting by Bernini of Pluto carrying a struggling Persephone over his shoulders. A pigeon landed on Pluto's head, then darted down to retrieve one of our bread crumbs and flew away.

We finished our lunch and walked along the belvedere. Clouds were coming in all around us. Lake Pergusa wasn't visible and Mount Etna had disappeared. Even the craggy rocks of Calascibetta and the Madonie Mountains were barely distinct. In this fortified place, it was easy to see how Enna's oldest known people, the Sicani, had been able to resist the advances of the warring Siculi, who had come from eastern Sicily in 3000 B.C. Then, as agriculture prospered in the valley below Enna, the Sicani had introduced a Great Mother cult that later, when the Greeks arrived, had been incorporated into the cult of Demeter and Persephone.

I walked with Barbara to the station to see her off. She gave me all her photocopies and some guidebooks before she climbed aboard the bus.

"Good luck with your search!" she called from the window. I was sorry to see her go.

The bus pulled out and headed down the steep, winding road. Walking slowly back through town, I looked in some shops, then went over to Piazza Marconi where I could see the church doors, now standing open. I crossed the square and went in.

As my eyes adjusted to the darkness, I saw that no one

else was inside. Glowing in the shadows, bits of gold leaf were like beacons, lighting up the stations of the cross that lined the walls of the nave, glimmering on the ceiling, or highlighting details of the statues. In the front was a simple altar, and I walked up to it quietly. On it was a marble statue of a Madonna with a halo around her head that looked like a giant scallop shell. Around her feet were small ex-voto photographs, and in her arms was the infant Christ. It didn't surprise me that it was a very ordinary Madonna. I hadn't really expected statues of Greek gods.

Nevertheless, I looked for pagan references. The shell, perhaps. This was an age-old fertility symbol, reminiscent of the Greek Aphrodite and her birth from the half-shell. The shell was also a Christian symbol of pilgrimage, which seemed appropriate for me considering how far I had come.

"*Signora*, may I help you?" A wrinkled old man appeared from the sacristy. Apparently a custodian, he carried a dust cloth. Walking slowly, he was stooped over, probably from working for years in this church. Before I could answer, he began pointing out the altar's rococo grillwork, the fancy pulpit, and even naming the artists who had made the stations of the cross. Coming full circle, his eyes rested on the altar. He was quiet for a moment.

"I was wondering, *signore*, about this altar. I have heard that, a hundred years ago, some Greek gods stood here. Is this true?"

He looked at me, surprised, then spoke in a low voice as if not wanting to be overhead.

"Oh, yes, not many people remember this. But my grandmother told me about it."

"Do you know which gods they were?" I asked.

"*Signora*, they were not gods," he said, whispering. "They were goddesses."

"Goddesses? *Sì?*" I was excited.

"Oh, yes. They were the statues of the great Demetra, holding her daughter, Proserpina."

I was amazed. Demeter and Persephone? Even though Enna was dedicated to these deities, I had somehow expected male gods to be on the altar.

"But when the pope found out, he made the people take the statues down," the old man continued, his voice even quieter. He looked fondly at this new statue standing in the old one's place. "Now we have the Madonna and her child. But to me, it is the same thing."

Then I noticed something on the altar. In front of the statue was a small plastic pot of sprouting wheat. It was similar to the wheat offerings I had seen women bring to a church near Trapani during Holy Week. These "Gardens of Adonis" were descended from the worship of Adonis, a god connected with fertility, death, and resurrection, once revered in Grecian settlements and throughout the Near East. Adonis had gone into Hades, a journeying lover-son like Osiris of the Egyptians or like Christ. But few realized that the cult of Adonis had evolved, through the centuries, from the Babylonian myth of the underworld visit made by the goddess, Inanna, an ancestress of Demeter and Persephone.

I looked at the photographs, propped around the statue's base, of sick children or petitioning parents. They reminded me of Dad's picture in Carolina's grave; the statue was like the sweet Madonnas to whom Carolina herself had prayed.

"You must pray every day to Mary," Grandmother had admonished me when she visited us in Oregon.

With the Hummel-style statue of Mary she had given me, I would kneel down to say my prayers at night in my attic bedroom. Certain that the attic was haunted, I was afraid to go to sleep. A safe passage through the darkness could only be ensured by saying the prayers in a certain superstitious order, as I had seen Grandmother do. It was

Photographs of the dead; Enna church.

exhausting to repeat some prayers three or perhaps seven times. If I didn't do it right, I was sure I would die as Jesus had, facing untold pain and suffering. I felt like the boy in the film *Equus*, but instead of a picture of a tormented Christ over my bed, I had the statue that Grandmother had given me.

Mary was my protectress, but later, as a teenager, I had sensed that she was trapped in the same Catholic world in which I struggled. It was a world of fear, of hell and death. God the Father was a punishing Yahweh, sending his own son to earth to die. Even the outcome of his crucifixion, the resurrection and eventual ascension into heaven, was upsetting. After facing all that suffering, Christ had said good-bye to his mother and apostles and disappeared. Then, a few years later, Mary had ascended into heaven, too.

Why hadn't she stayed on earth to help me? It was the least she could have done. Now that I was older, I wished Carolina were still around. Both these women knew about the domineering Yahweh and the suffering a mother experienced. But they weren't talking.

The silence in the church was deafening. The custodian lit a votive candle, his lips moving in prayer. It seemed time to go. I whispered my thanks and crept quietly away. At the door I turned to wave; now on his knees, he was still praying. But there was a naturalness about him, as if he were simply talking to the Madonna. After all these years he seemed to know her well.

Back at Piazza Marconi, half of Enna had come outside to begin the evening stroll, or *passeggiata*. Fathers pushed baby strollers; mothers walked alongside, in smart dresses and heels. Old men walked arm in arm with their wives or held the hands of grandchildren.

As I had in Trapani, I wondered how these families could be so contented. Or were they? Occasionally I would see a family man's eyes wander to a passing woman's swaying hips or catch a look of melancholy on a mother's face. I felt out of place and headed back toward Demeter's rock. The clouds had passed over Enna, and I hoped to spend an hour in solitude before my bus arrived.

My plans to be alone were dashed when I found the man with the car still waiting by the rock. He waved meekly but kept his distance, leaning against the car and smoking a cigarette. He watched me as I walked around the rock, climbed down, then back up again. I decided to take a photograph of the distant landscape, but it was impossible to find a view that didn't include the ugly iron railing. Finally I climbed onto the outcropping as I had before, balanced my tripod, and, watching the light change, photographed for nearly an hour.

The setting sun was turning Calascibetta, across the valley, a burning ocher. Mount Etna now soared up, distinctly visible; a glowing snowcap topped her peak. According to legend, Demeter had come here after Persephone had disappeared; now Sicilians said that when Etna exploded, it was "Demeter venting her wrath." A few years before, she'd had a spectacular eruption, spewing volcanic ash on the villages below. Through the centuries this was a common occurrence, and more than once, she had wiped out Catania at her base.

I climbed off the outcropping. The man was still watching me; now he left his car and came over. I ignored him and folded up my tripod.

"*Signora,* you were *una bella figura* on the rock. You work very hard to make a photo . . ."

"Yes," I nodded, now making a pretense of sorting out my bag.

"You are quite serious about this place of Demeter . . ."

"*Signore,*" I said, "excuse me. What time is it?" I had lost track of time in my preoccupation with photographing.

He showed me his watch. I panicked. The bus was

scheduled to leave in ten minutes. I grabbed my day pack, camera bag, and tripod and jumped off the rock.

"Where are you going? . . . *Signora!*"

"I'm late, I must catch a bus!" I said impatiently. I started running toward the station as he clamored after me.

"But I can take you there!"

"No!" I shouted and fled down the street.

It was about a mile to the station, and my bus was the last one for the day. If I missed it, I would be stuck in Enna for two days as tomorrow was Sunday and bus service was limited. I ran, crazed, through the streets. I prayed it would be late, but that was unlikely. Thanks to Mussolini, since the 1930s all of Italy had prided itself on trains and buses that ran on time.

I arrived breathlessly at the station; sure enough, the bus was just pulling out. I yelled and ran after it. The driver didn't see me. I swore in English, as the unconcerned stationmaster shrugged.

"Sorry, *signora,* what can I do?"

Just then, none other than the man from Demeter's rock pulled up in his car and screeched to a halt.

"*Signora,* get in. I will take you to catch the bus."

I looked at him, my hair a mess and perspiration dripping down my face.

"We must hurry. Get in!"

I hesitated, looking nervously around. The clouds were coming in again, and it would soon be night. I wanted to get back to Trapani. I looked at him again.

"Well . . . I could pay you . . ." I offered.

"No, *signora.* I would not think of it. But come, we must go!"

Without thinking further, I jumped in, and we were off.

I slumped exhausted into the seat. The man looked over at me. His white teeth flashed in a big grin. "Allow me to introduce myself," he said. "My name is Roberto."

He screeched down the precipitous road. What had I

done? Thoughts of my mother's "Be careful" at the Palermo train station came back to me. I remembered accounts of local rapes and murders, now convinced I would be the first *americana* to turn up missing somewhere in central Sicily.

I kept my hand on the door handle, prepared to jump out at the first sign of an attack from Roberto. We tore down the mountain road, careening onto the shoulder on the hairpin turns. We narrowly missed an oncoming car. I pleaded with Roberto to slow down, but he seemed to accelerate. I felt like Persephone descending into Hades with Pluto—except that I had gone by choice.

We caught sight of the bus, cutting a wide berth around the turns five hundred feet below us. Now I wanted Roberto to speed up, but instead, he seemed to slow down.

"Hurry!" I urged him. "We must catch it!"

He ignored me and slowed down to a crawl. Then he pulled over onto a side road and stopped. I was sure I was doomed and grabbed the door handle. He looked over at me and sighed.

"I'm sorry. I think there is something wrong with the car."

He jumped out and opened the hood. I wondered at first if it were a ruse, but his tinkering seemed to be in earnest. He pulled on the spark plugs. He was hurrying now and kept pausing from his work to look down the mountain for the bus.

Finally he climbed back into the car and announced that it was fixed. The engine started up, sputtered, then the car lurched onto the pavement with a jump. We were off again.

I closed my eyes as he sped down the road, recklessly passing the oncoming traffic.

"Don't worry, we will make it," he said, trying to console me. He smiled contentedly, then squinted at the switch-backing road below us. He pointed out his window. "There it is again—the bus!"

Persephone's abduction, terra-cotta frieze, 500 B.C., found at Locri, Italy; National Museum of Reggio Calabria.

It must have been the first time in Sicilian history that a bus had gone so fast. We traveled ten more miles like this, honking and waving, and were soon in the valley. It was dark and the lights of a town appeared up ahead. Finally the bus pulled over to let some passengers off. We drove up behind it with a great screech.

"*Un momento*. Wait here," said Roberto. He jumped out and ran over to the bus driver, whom he seemed to know. I saw Roberto hand him some money.

I got out and ran over to the driver and Roberto, with money for the ticket in my hand.

"No." Roberto pushed the money away. "It is already paid for."

"Please, you must not do that," I insisted.

"No. It is my privilege." He smiled sweetly, then grabbed my bags and helped me onto the bus.

I stood in the doorway, looking at him. Finally I reached out my hand. "Thank you," I said, overwhelmed. "*Grazie tanto.*"

"It is nothing," he said. He was silent for a moment. "Tell me," he asked, "did you find your goddesses up there in Enna?"

I smiled and thought for a moment. "Well, yes, I think I did."

I took my seat. My fine Pluto waved and then drove off into the night.

CHAPTER IV

Lucia's Kitchen

WHEN I RETURNED TO Trapani from Enna, I found Carlo at the pensione. Tom, the boys, and Mother had returned from Selinunte and Palermo that afternoon, just in time to accept an invitation from Carlo.

"My mother wants you all to come for dinner," said Carlo. "And, Susanna, if you like, she will teach you how to make couscous."

A Sicilian woman was actually asking us to her home! And the proposed couscous lesson was a rare opportunity to learn how Sicily's popular Arab dish was made. I smiled at Carlo's obvious desire to teach me domestic skills. I knew he would rather see me cooking than scurrying about the island looking for goddesses in caves.

How had we wrangled this invitation? I wondered. During the preceding week I had asked Carlo and Giuseppe questions about their mothers, especially during dinner on Holy Thursday. But they had not answered me directly, speaking about their mothers in hushed tones, almost as if they were sacred. Their homes, I had assumed, were clearly off limits to strangers. Had I proved myself by becoming so involved and interested in the procession? Or perhaps Carlo had seen a different side of me during our hike across Levanzo. Somehow, he had now decided that it was safe to bring us home.

He returned a few hours later to drive us to his house. We all squeezed into his little car and drove toward New Trapani. On the way he played tapes on his car stereo. One was of Afro-pop music he had bought in Nairobi, where his ship had docked once; the other was the Beatles' *Let It Be*, to which Carlo knew the English words. As he sang the lines about Mother Mary appearing in times of trouble, I was surprised by its religious reference. Although I'd listened to the song many times, I'd never realized until now that it was about the Madonna.

"Do you know it?" he asked.

I nodded. Carlo said that he and his friends loved the Beatles' music; many Sicilians did, in fact. Especially this song.

"Let it be," he sang in his strong voice, leading us in the chorus, which even Mother sang with us, as we zoomed along the curving seafront. We had traced Trapani's sickle shape from its tip nearly to the base when Carlo turned into a neighborhood of postwar houses and drove up to a large building on Via Verona.

"And now you meet Lucia—my mother," Carlo announced as he parked and came around to open the car door for us. I looked around me as I got out; children paused from their soccer game on the street to watch us, and old women peered out of windows, wondering who these invaders of their street were.

I braced myself as we entered the building and walked up through two locked doors to the darkened third floor. After all the innuendos and hushed tones that Carlo had used when speaking about his mother, I felt that I was rendezvousing with the Blessed Virgin herself.

Lucia was waiting at the top of the stairs. Carlo was

At the window.

almost shy as he introduced us. She grinned, showing a mouth full of gaps and an occasional sparkling gold tooth. She was surprisingly friendly and reminded me a little of my grandmother, but with curly hair. She wore an over- sized apron, like Carolina's, over a green sweater and black skirt. She was comfortably stout, with sturdy legs encased in heavy nylon stockings. Her feet were swollen, as older Italian women's often are, and they seemed too big for her worn black shoes, which looked like slippers.

She was probably the same age as my mother, though she looked fifteen years older. I had hoped that she and Mother would have something in common, but Lucia's at- tention was focused on me.

"Come in," she urged, taking my hand. "I'm beginning the couscous now." She pulled me into the kitchen while Carlo led the others into the dining room.

It was a tiny, fastidious kitchen with a very small sink and minuscule counter space; I remembered Carolina cooking in a similar place when Dad had taken me to visit her in New Jersey. The kitchens of working-class families were always scrupulously clean like this. Perhaps the women cleaned and scrubbed to erase their peasant past, still too close for comfort, and to bring their families, by sheer force of broom and sponge, into the middle class. But, as I had noticed at my grandmother's, in these im- maculate spaces culinary miracles could occur.

To complete this setting, a man sat at a wooden table, reminding me of how often I had seen Grandpa Antonio sit watching Carolina. This man was so quiet that I barely noticed him at first. Lucia introduced him as her husband, Mario, who, she said, had been a *portatore* like Carlo for many years. A glass of homemade wine sat in front of him on the table; he smiled broadly as he got up to pour an- other from a five-gallon bottle on the floor. He offered the glass to me but poured none for Lucia; then he insisted I sit down. He settled down again himself, occasionally stealing a glance at a small television set on the counter.

Mario was totally comfortable in this womblike space; when Lucia heaved a ten-pound cloth sack onto the table, he moved politely over to a chair in the kitchen's corner. I got up and stood behind Lucia. The sack contained semolina, she explained. The tiny grains were a farina-like Italian cereal and the primary ingredient for couscous.

"First you must sift them," instructed Lucia, thrusting her strong hands into the golden grain. "Like this." Then she slowly added handfuls of the semolina to a small amount of water contained in a large bowl. "Now you must blend it with the tips of your fingers."

She wanted me to try it. I did, and it seemed easy.

"No, no. Not with the heel of your hand—the tips."

I tried again, but Lucia frowned. "No, no: the tips!" admonished Lucia impatiently. The kitchen door opened and Mother came in to watch.

"Let Mama try it," said Lucia.

Mother did and performed the movement perfectly. Lucia smiled.

"I think your mama understands these things," she said, matter-of-factly.

I felt like a failure. I tried again and still, according to Lucia, I couldn't do it. Mother now laughed, which upset me even more. I wanted to endear myself to Lucia, but how could I if, according to her standards, I was an inept housewife? Carlo came in and chided me, as did his father. What kind of woman was I, they seemed to wonder, if I couldn't mix a few grain seeds together?

Mother and Carlo left the room. Lucia and I continued, adding pepper, onions, garlic, and olive oil to the semolina. Then we blended it together with our hands. This was easier, and now Lucia was happy. We put the whole mixture into an earthenware pot with holes, a "couscous cooker," which Lucia set on top of a panful of water on the stove. In the meanwhile, she began to make a tomato sauce that would be served with the couscous, as well as a fish broth that would be added to the cooked semolina.

She attended to the steaming mixture. "You must keep it clumped together," warned Lucia, folding the grain with a fork. "Then you must seal the cooker." She rolled out coils of dough with her hands and pressed them around the seam between the cooker and the pan of water. This, she explained, would keep the air out so that the mixture could steam. With the dough and double-decker earthenware pots, the construction looked like a two-story Arab mosque.

All we needed to do now was wait for it to cook, said Lucia. She did the cleanup, refusing to let me help and motioning to the table, where I sat down with Mario. The pots gurgled on the stove, and I thought of similar scenes in Grandmother Carolina's kitchen, watching her make pizza or delicious mounds of fried doughnuts that she would sprinkle with sugar to tempt us kids. I relished Italian cooking. When I would visit my parents' house, it was a pleasure to watch as Mother and Dad—who actually liked to cook—prepared elaborate Italian stews or mixed salads with greens that I couldn't name. Their kitchen was a comforting space; I felt similarly comforted now, gazing at Lucia. She interrupted her cleaning to fret over the coil of dough on the couscous cooker, which had come loose. I tried to help but once more she waved me away; Mario pounded on the table, eager for me to sit down again, and refilled my glass of wine.

Carlo came in a few minutes later. He wanted to show me the rest of the house. First we went into the dining room, which had lacy white curtains and shiny marble floors. A crucifix and prints of alpine landscapes were on the walls, and little shelves contained mementos: dolls, religious statues, a decorative bottle of Galliano in the shape of an Italian carabiniere. At the big table, which was covered with an embroidered tablecloth, Tom sat uncomfortably in a hard-backed chair. The boys greedily stuffed themselves from a tray of sweets. Mother sat on a couch and smiled, trying to make conversation in Italian with Mario, who had sat down next to her.

Then my tour continued down the hallway. Carlo motioned to a room belonging to his sister, who was visiting her fiancé's family that night. Then he opened the door at the end of the hallway. "This is my room," he said, urging me in. I had thought this would be forbidden territory to a female guest, but Carlo was insistent. It was a tidy room, just like the rest of the house. In the corner was a tiny single bed; I wondered how Carlo could fit into it, considering his size. There was a small television on a bookshelf, which had no books. A small dresser was topped by a doily upon which was a statue of Saint Anthony. There was a picture of Carlo's mother in a frame by the bed and a painting of the Madonna on the wall. It was difficult to think of him spending time in such a feminine room. It didn't look lived in, but on second thought I guessed it wasn't, considering the amount of time Carlo spent in Old Town with his friends.

Who, in fact, arrived just then. After a knock on the front door, in walked Giuseppe and two carriers of the *Ceto del Popolo*. One was a swarthy man I called "Carlo Misterioso," to differentiate between him and Carlo Sugameli and because, with his dark mustache and gold jewelry, he reminded me of a stereotypical mafioso. The other was a stout young man named Salvatore. Apparently, they were to join us for dinner. We all assembled in the dining room while Lucia, in the kitchen, fretted over the couscous. We sat around the table as Mario brought out glasses and some unopened bottles of whiskey he had bought just for us. Carlo's *portatori* friends, still euphoric from carrying the *Misteri*, were happy to see Tom again and, pouring him a generous shot, began to reminisce about the procession.

Mario joined in, telling of his days as a porter. At first the conversation's tone was solemn, while everyone drank and smoked cigarettes. But then it became animated as, each time the glasses were refilled, someone would toast with "Ciao" or "Chin-chin." From around the huge table, we all made an effort to clink our glasses together.

"To Tommaso, the *bilancino!*" said Carlo Misterioso.

"To Sky, *un bravo regazzo*," proclaimed Giuseppe, looking fondly at Sky. Then he winked at Shane, who was sitting on my lap. "And next time, if his mother allows, Shane must march in the procession, too."

Lucia appeared, interrupting the merrymaking. She asked me what kind of pasta I would like for our meal. I was surprised. Couscous *and* pasta at the same meal?

"Oh, anything, Lucia. We'll like whatever you make."

"But what kind of food do you like in America?" she insisted.

"Everything . . . spicy things . . ."

"Hamburgers?" said Carlo. "Hot dogs?" He teased.

"Yes. Or Mexican food. I love the chilies!"

Lucia thought a moment, then disappeared back into the kitchen.

Everyone was half-intoxicated when Lucia came out again to set the table. The liquor bottles were swept to one side to make room for the antipasto.

It was delicious: a marinated eggplant dish and the usual olives, cheese, and bread. This alone was a meal. The kids stuffed themselves, but I knew that more was coming and restrained myself. Carlo and his friends finished and lit cigarettes, savoring the time before the next course. Soon Lucia cleared the antipasto plates and brought in the spaghetti, covered in a grainy, bright red sauce. Carlo tasted it, then turned up his nose.

"Mama, what is this?" he asked.

I tasted it. The spaghetti was in a tomato-based sauce that had been well spiked with an Italian-made chili powder. To please me, Lucia had apparently prepared "*spaghetti alla mexicana.*" It was very spicy and strange tasting, but I felt obliged to eat it. Mario and the *portatori* were embarrassed and picked at their plates, watching me as I feigned pleasure at the odd concoction.

Then came the couscous. Lucia ladled the lumpy, steaming mass into bowls that were our third set of dinnerware; I cringed at the thought of the dishwashing that would follow this meal. She poured the fish broth on top, setting a side dish of tomato sauce on the table. Though I was already full, I dutifully plunged in.

"*Mangia,*" said Lucia, finally sitting down herself. She grinned, her gold teeth flashing, and urged us to eat. "*Mangia!*"

The couscous was delicious and obviously a delight to Carlo's family and the *portatori.* They all had several helpings. The tiny semolina grains made it fluffy and light; it reminded me of a delicate Arab script.

"*Buono,*" I said to Lucia.

"*Buono,*" she agreed and polished her plate.

It wasn't over yet. There followed a salad, drenched in olive oil, of *radicchio,* or wild chicory leaves, and tomatoes. The plates were cleared again. As if this weren't enough, we were then treated to a fancy Easter cake, made in the shape of a dove, and to after-dinner liqueurs, including a bottle of cognac that Carlo Misterioso had brought.

I was ready to go back to the pensione by now. Tom and I exchanged tired glances, but the evening seemed to have entered a second phase. Carlo refilled our glasses with cognac. The *portatori* began reliving the procession again, drinking and puffing on cigarettes and cigars that Mario passed around, until the dining room resembled a smoke-filled poolroom. The children were asleep at the table; it was late. Lucia, Tom, and I carried them into Carlo's bedroom.

I thought Lucia would go to bed now herself, but she

returned and sat quietly by Mother at the end of the table. As the men became rowdier, she grew even quieter. At one point I thought she had fallen asleep in her chair. But she stirred, raised her head, and smiled at all of us. Then her head dropped again. The conversation grew louder, but it was difficult to follow, for now the *portatori* spoke a rapid Sicilian. It sounded like they were talking about the Madonna's entrance into the church, Carlo saying something about her platform almost tipping. Suddenly Giuseppe stood up, girlishly clutched his hands to his breast, fluttered his eyes, and pretended to fall. It was a hilarious imitation of the Madonna. The two Carlos and Mario jumped up, doubling over in laughter.

"Here, get up here!" Salvatore removed the glasses and bottles from the table and pounded on it. Tom, Mother, and I got out of our chairs, wondering what was happening now.

Salvatore and Carlo Misterioso picked up Giuseppe and laid him, struggling, on the table. Lucia woke up with a start, shook her head, then got up to stand in the doorway.

Carlo excitedly grabbed a dishcloth and draped it over Giuseppe's head like a veil. Giuseppe lay seductively on the table, propped up on his elbow with his free hand clutching his heart and his eyes and mouth squeezed into a pained expression. Salvatore took some plastic flowers out of a nearby vase and arranged them at Giuseppe's feet.

"*La Madonna!*" The *portatori* were howling. Giuseppe grimaced even more, then pretended to fall off the table.

All the men, including Mario and Tom, who had now joined them, kicked the chairs out of the way, then squatted at the table's four corners in their carrying position. "*Al posto!*" commanded Carlo. With Giuseppe bouncing around on top, they picked the table up and began to carry it around the small room. Lucia watched from the doorway as if she had seen this event many times before. Mother and I stood in the corner, amazed.

"Bum, bum, ba-bum, bum, ba-bum . . . BUM . . . BA-BUM . . . bum!" began Carlo, humming *"Vela,"* a dirge from the procession. Giuseppe sighed and moaned with great drama from the tabletop and pretended to plunge a kitchen knife, which Salvatore had handed him, into his chest.

The room proved too small for their procession. They headed toward the doorway to the hall, as Lucia ducked aside. It was a tight fit. Lucia held her breath as the table scraped the door's molding, and then the men gleefully proceeded down the hallway toward Carlo's room. They carried the teetering table back, then went down the hall again. There were only inches to spare between the table and the walls. A picture fell off the wall. Lucia, alarmed and preferring not to look, retreated to the kitchen.

The laughing *portatori*, still assisted by Tom, edged the table and Giuseppe back through the doorway and deposited them in the dining room with a thud. Giuseppe lay on the table, still clutching his breast and pretending he was dead.

"Basta! Enough!" shouted the returning Lucia. Exasperated, she shook her head at the clowning men. Giuseppe climbed off the table; Carlo, still laughing, helped his mother reset it with the bottles and glasses. The chairs were put back, and we all sat down again. It had been quite a show.

Carlo and the *portatori* poured another round of drinks and talked softly. I was exhausted. When, I wondered, would someone take us back to the pensione? It seemed impolite to ask. Lucia sat by herself at the table's end.

It was very quiet now. Suddenly Lucia, in an almost inaudible voice, began to hum. It sounded like a lullaby, a tune that she would use to put a child to sleep. Gradually she raised her voice. Everyone turned to listen to her words: *"E si misiru a caminari san Giuvanni cu Maria, San Giuvanni cu Maria e 'ncuntraru na putta . . ."*

It was a Sicilian song about the seven sorrows of the Virgin Mary. All eyes focused on Lucia as she sang. I thought of the *Madonna Addolorata* and the seven daggers in her heart, representing her sorrows: being separated from Christ, seeing him fall under the cross, his crucifixion, and so on.

I remembered Grandmother and the times I had heard her sing like this.

"Susan," my younger sisters Angela and Shawn would say, their eyes opened wide, "Grandma is singing!" We would peek around a corner and listen in fascination. She might have been rolling out pasta dough or making beds when she would break out in spontaneous song. She had a strange, high-pitched, almost scary voice. They seemed like sad songs, although we didn't know what they meant. But we knew they were religious because of all the "Maria's" and "Jesu's."

Grandmother's songs were resurrected in Lucia's, which was a tale of the Madonna's broken heart. But it was ageless in its anguish; it could have been Demeter's lament for Persephone. Lucia, for these moments, was shaking off the cloak of propriety that she wore. And I couldn't help thinking that it wasn't just a lost or wayward son she mourned but also a lost part of herself.

Lucia droned on, in a voice that was almost pretty, through all the verses. The song ended abruptly, and she looked down. The men seemed impressed yet a little uneasy. Had Lucia been singing about them and their playacting?

Lucia broke the silence. "It is time to sleep. Susanna, you must all stay here tonight." I tried to refuse. How could she sleep all of us in her apartment? "No, please," she said. She turned to Mother. "We can fix a bed here in the dining room for you and the boys."

Then she turned to Tom and me. "And you can sleep in my bed. Mario and I can use my daughter's room."

Cross; Lucia's house.

I protested again, but it was no use. Mario busied himself with unfolding the couch in the dining room, and Carlo went to his room to get the boys. Salvatore, Giuseppe, and Carlo Misterioso kissed all of us good-bye and left.

Lucia ushered Tom and me into her room. She kissed both of us good night and closed the door.

We were in an eerie inner sanctum, like a church. The room was dark, lit only by a votive light on the dresser, which illuminated a statue of the Virgin Mary. On a small table was a glow-in-the-dark statue of Saint Francis of Paula. A broken crucifix was on the wall.

I shivered. It was like going to bed in Grandmother's room. I remembered the mixed feelings I had had when, as a child, I had slept in the same bed with Carolina. Now she was present again in Lucia. I was honored, in a way, to have been given this room; its massive bed and cold marble floors made it a chamber fit for a high priestess. But it was also like a church, and I knew that, on this night, a dark and restless woman slept there, her search still incomplete.

CHAPTER V

Clara's Restaurant

"SUSANNA, THERE'S SOMEONE HERE to see you," called Pina, knocking on my door. I opened it softly, and Pina motioned toward the foyer; it was my last night in Trapani, and I had a final dinner engagement. I picked up my jacket, said good-bye to Tom, who was staying behind with the boys, and went out into the foyer. Pina peered curiously from the hallway. She must have been wondering what I was up to now. There had been so much craziness in the past month, with the comings and goings of this *americana* and her entourage.

Gian Carlo sat waiting on the couch. He was stylishly dressed in a tan overcoat and a long, bright blue scarf. He was about thirty-five, his hair prematurely streaked with gray. His bushy eyebrows, resembling those of the Mexican painter Frida Kahlo, grew together and gave his deep-set eyes an owlish, ponderous look. Though he seemed too young to be one, he was a practicing psychiatrist with offices in both Trapani and Palermo. I wondered how a Sicilian psychiatrist was supposed to appear. It was difficult to match looks and occupation in Sicily. There were Sicilian priests with red hair and even mafiosi, I was finding, who did not look like the movie characters or like Carlo Misterioso. The few I had seen were dressed conservatively, like bookkeepers or bank tellers.

"Sorry I'm late," said Gian Carlo, who spoke perfect English, learned when he had gone to school in the States. "We're going to I Trabanesi, a restaurant you'll like very much. There is someone I want you to meet. And," he added, "I want to hear all about your experiences in Sicily."

He, too, was interested in mythology and folklore. I had met him in the church on Holy Saturday when the *ceti* were being disassembled. Guessing that I was American, he had come up to introduce himself. With his blue smock and beret, it had been obvious that he was a *portatore*, but I had been surprised when he said that he was also a doctor; *portatori* were usually working-class men. We had briefly discussed the procession, and Gian Carlo's eyes had lit up when I mentioned my theories about its pre-Christian roots. He had seemed to know quite a bit about the subject. Wanting to continue our conversation, we had quickly exchanged phone numbers. As it turned out, he had some appointments in Trapani on the last day before our departure and had called that morning to invite me to dinner.

We walked east on the Corso, away from Trapani's tip, then cut through a side street that led toward the old Jewish quarter. We were now in a maze of tiny, narrow alleys, a section of Old Town I hadn't seen before. We passed a grim-looking neoclassic building, sandwiched between two crumbling apartment flats.

"That is the library," pointed out Gian Carlo. It looked gloomy and deserted, as if no one ever used it.

"My friend Clara," he said, "the woman who runs I Trabanesi, spent many years there poring over books. She was working on a university thesis."

"Oh? What was she studying?" I asked. This sounded

Street-corner shrine; old Jewish quarter, Trapani.

unusual for Trapani: a woman restaurateur who was also a scholar.

"You'll never guess," he said, shuddering in the wind that had suddenly risen from the port. He tucked his scarf closer around his neck.

"What?" I asked. "The history of Sicily since fascism?" Gian Carlo laughed. "Tell me," I said.

"It was about the Procession of the Mysteries," he finally said.

I looked at him, surprised.

"Yes," he said, guiding me through a narrow passageway. He glanced at me, his eyes twinkling. "She's the person I want you to meet. Clara was studying the procession's roots, like you." We were now out of the dark maze of narrow streets and in a little piazza. Just ahead, I saw a small sign on a building. It was the restaurant.

I was surprised that a Trapani woman had researched the procession. Most Sicilians rarely analyzed the procession; they simply responded to it with their emotions. I thought of the library, imagining all the fragile manuscripts available to this Clara. And her Italian, surely better than mine, would have allowed her insights into medieval treatises, histories of the Trapani trade guilds, accounts from the Bourbon Spanish . . .

"What did she find out?" I asked.

"That," said Gian Carlo, "I do not know."

He opened the restaurant's door. It was a small place, filled with people sitting banquet style at several long tables. The decor was unusual for a Sicilian restaurant. Instead of majolica pottery or travel posters, the walls held lithographs and paintings that reminded me of artwork we students had produced during graduate school. It was the first time I had seen any fine art in Sicily. The clientele wasn't the usual, either. Gian Carlo greeted a table full of men with slightly long hair and eccentric clothes. They looked like artists. But most unusual was the preponderance of women in the restaurant. Young, student types sat with some of the men. One group of middle-aged women sitting by the door appeared to be local housewives out for an evening together, unescorted by men.

We sat down and I continued an account of my adventures over the past few weeks. Gian Carlo was curious about the paintings in the Levanzo cave, which he had never seen; then he laughed at the frightening ride I had taken with Roberto down the road from Enna. Mostly, I complained about the difficulty I had had traveling alone. Gian Carlo thought for a moment, searching for an explanation.

"It has always been this way in Sicily for women." He looked at the menu. "I think you can find the answer right here. Look." He pointed to listings of couscous dishes, spaghetti with eggplant sauce, and desserts made with pistachios or ground-up almonds.

"These are Arab dishes. Most people forget that the Moors lived here for four hundred years." He looked at me. "I think, in many ways, Sicily is still an Arab society."

I thought of the mosques I had seen in Palermo and of the Arab-Norman arches that graced Trapani's architecture. I remembered Lucia's couscous cooking lesson.

"Remember," continued Gian Carlo, "the Arabs kept women inside. Our architecture still reflects this, with apartments walled to the street and with inner courtyards. That is where the Sicilian women are, in the harem." He laughed.

Just then a woman of about forty came over. She had short dark hair and wore jeans and low, comfortable shoes. A pair of glasses attached to a chain dangled from her neck. She hugged Gian Carlo, then sat down between us. Gian Carlo introduced us: this was Clara.

She nodded at me with interest but said nothing. I wanted to ask her questions about the procession, but her mind seemed to be on other matters. In a low husky voice she described the restaurant's specialties for the night. I was fascinated at how deliberately she described each item, right down to the individual herbs used in a sauce for lamb or to the region of Sicily from which the cheeses had been procured for the tortellini. It was a cooking lesson conducted by a scholar, and the nuances in her voice were as subtle and varied as the complexities of Sicilian life and food themselves.

She was obviously a true *siciliana*, in love with food. Almost reverently, she and Gian Carlo selected the items we would eat. Then, explaining that there had been little help in the kitchen all afternoon, she looked around at the full tables and announced she had to get back.

Soon she returned, bringing sausage and pepper antipasto, followed by spaghetti and a main course of the lamb sautéed in a delicate fennel sauce. A little while later, she returned to sit with us. I complimented her on the meal; between the variety of items on her menu and the potpourri of sauces, herbs, and spices, she had offered the best food I had eaten in Sicily.

She smiled, eager to explain. "It is the food of *le barone*," she said. "The old barons of Sicily were world travelers, and they mixed with the many cultures that were here."

She looked around proudly at her clientele. "I want to bring a taste of Sicily's past to these people."

Finally the conversation turned to my travel experiences. Gian Carlo listened quietly, then told Clara of my tribulations while traveling alone.

She laughed, as Gian Carlo had. "I know these problems well." She glanced around the room again, gesturing toward the tables of women. "That is why I have this restaurant," she explained.

I wondered what she meant.

"For instance, women hardly ever go out to eat alone. But they will come here. I try to make the food beautiful to them and to welcome them when they come in. They feel comfortable here because a woman runs the restaurant."

"So in this way you are bringing them outside?"

"Yes." She seemed pleased that I understood. "That's exactly it."

I was eager to hear about Clara's university thesis. What had she uncovered about the procession's pre-Christian roots?

"There are writings of the Middle Ages that hint at certain mysterious fertility rites occurring here before Christianity. But it is hard to know just what they were."

"What about the Greeks and even before them?"

"Well, you know that Trapani is named after the goddess, Demeter?"

"What do you mean?"

"Trapani's first name was Drepanum, a Greek word meaning scythe. The story is that Demeter dropped her sickle here when she went to look for Persephone, and the distinctive shape of Trapani was formed."

I was surprised. Here was a name for Trapani associated with Demeter, whereas the Christian name denoted a black cloth signifying funerals. One signified fertility, the other death. The ideas seemed contradictory.

I asked Clara what her impressions of the procession were this year. She looked at Gian Carlo and they were soon talking in a rapid-fire Italian that I couldn't understand.

Gian Carlo paused to include me. "We're talking about the *Ceto Salinai,* the *ceto* of the salt workers' guild. Clara carries for them in the procession, you know."

"The whole distance?" I asked.

"Yes," said Clara, nonchalantly. "I have been doing it for three years now."

The restaurant was now mobbed with late-nighters, and Clara excused herself to return to the kitchen.

I wanted to ask Gian Carlo more about this sudden revelation. A woman actually shouldering the *Misteri* in the procession? It was hard to believe. But he was quiet, as if Clara's carrying were a private matter, which he respected and felt he shouldn't discuss. We finished our dessert, then went back to the kitchen to say good-bye to Clara.

Tomato sauce was splattered on her apron, and she was stirring a huge pot of pasta. She set the spoon down on the stove to embrace Gian Carlo, then reached out her arms to me, too.

"Ciao . . . and thank you. *Grazie tanto,*" I said. "I'm leaving for America tomorrow . . . I wish we could talk some more."

"We will see each other again." She peered into my eyes. "You will come back." She seemed to know something that I didn't. "If you do, come find me. We can go to the procession together."

Then Clara returned to her cooking, and we left.

On the way back, I wondered about Clara's invitation: was it real or just a form of politeness? I liked Clara and was frustrated at having to leave for the States the next day, when I had just met her. But I didn't feel I belonged here, either. I was worlds away from Gian Carlo and Clara and their connection, through the procession, to the Trapani community. Yet I wanted a similar connection in my own life.

At the pensione, I sadly said good-bye to Gian Carlo, promising to keep in touch, then went upstairs to do some last-minute packing. The next morning Carlo Sugameli helped us load all our bags into his car so that he could take us to the train station. We thanked Pina, who walked with us out to the street; then we piled in for the brief ride.

"One moment," said Carlo. "My mother wants to say good-bye." He took a detour along the waterfront and soon pulled up at his apartment. As before, all the neighbors were watching. Carlo led me out of the car while my family stayed inside. We walked up to the third floor where Lucia

Lucia's neighbor.

was waiting. I hugged her, expressing my gratitude for everything. She told me that she had a surprise and asked me to close my eyes. Then she thrust a heavy ten-pound bag into my arms.

"It is semolina, for couscous. You must learn to cook."

I laughed through misted eyes. "I will try."

"Do not forget us!" she shouted, as Carlo and I ran back down the stairs.

Of course I would not forget. But would they forget me? I looked up at Lucia, now waving from her balcony. I patted the bag of semolina as though it were a baby. Understanding my antics, she forced a laugh as I had seen Carolina do so many times. How would I get this heavy bag back to America? I wondered. Lucia looked like a sad grain goddess, a distraught Demeter, with yet another child disappearing. From her window, she could only watch me go. I thought of Clara, the other important woman I had met. She was like Persephone, the one in the myth who obviously got "out." She seemed to be on an important journey, one that I wanted to share, yet I still couldn't define it for myself. I felt caught between these women; I was not one, nor was I the other.

The train was waiting at the station, and Carlo and Tom loaded all our bags into a second-class compartment. We even had a five-gallon plastic jug of local wine, given to us by Giuseppe the day before, on which Sky had comically written *vino*. Mother got the boys settled as Tom and I sat down with Carlo for a moment. I felt wordless at parting and on the verge of tears.

"You are like my brother and sister," Carlo said. "Like family. If you come back, our house is yours."

Then the train's whistle sounded and Carlo jumped off. I stood at the doorway, watching him and Trapani's little station vanish behind us.

I was openly crying now. It was as if I had held back these tears for days. The other passengers stared. Mother and Tom were embarrassed; they couldn't understand this emotion. I couldn't really understand it myself.

"But, Susan," said Mother, "you've got a wonderful story to write when you get back: the procession, Sky walking in it, the cave, Enna. You found so much."

Yes, I thought through my tears. But what she didn't realize was that I had just barely begun. I didn't want to leave; there was so much left to find.

CHAPTER VI

In the Harem

WITH TWO TRIPS TO Sicily behind me, I felt increasingly dissatisfied with my life in Oregon. I was full of memories of Trapani's procession and the warmth of people like Lucia, Carlo, and Giuseppe. I missed the Sicilian food and wine and wanted to live, like the Mediterraneans, surrounded by history and antiquity. I envied Clara and Gian Carlo and their yearly participation in the procession. I wanted ritual in my life, too, and a theater in which to act out the full range of my emotions: grief, love, hope, fear. But there were no rituals in America, nothing that acted on me deeply or that invited my participation. How pale the westernized Easter of the following year seemed in comparison to Trapani's procession. But my friends looked at me blankly when I raved about Good Friday in Sicily. I think most of them assumed that I had undergone some kind of religious conversion.

Perhaps I had. And the strange thing was, in having glimpsed an "underworld" in Sicily and a Madonna who dared to visit it while others were denied this journey by a two-thousand-year-old patriarchy, I suddenly found myself catapulted into a frightening dark place of my own.

It started with nights of insomnia, not long after I returned. I would wake with a palpitating heart, unable to fall back asleep, no matter what remedy I tried. Then one day, while standing under the shadowless fluorescent lights illuminating a supermarket checkout line, I gazed uncomfortably at the thousands of Brillo boxes, Gothic paperbacks, Wheat Chex specials, and *National Enquirers* around me. Suddenly, my whole world caved in. I couldn't stand to be there; I felt dizzy, and the store spun around me. Things looked unfamiliar as I stared, unable to speak, at the checkout clerk. I felt I couldn't walk and was sure that everyone in the store was watching me; I fumbled with my money, half of it landing on the counter and the rest on the floor. Mumbling something to the clerk, I bolted out of the store in confusion. I was in the middle of a full-blown panic attack.

Over the previous few years I had experienced several small episodes, early warning signals of this terrible panic. Sometimes in the middle of a conversation, I would suddenly feel distanced from it, as if I weren't there. I would lose my train of thought midsentence; things would become dreamlike and people would appear physically smaller, as if viewed through the wrong end of a telescope. But these derealizations had lasted only moments. I thought they were leftovers from my childhood, when I had had similar feelings that life was a dream from which I would soon wake up. I remembered those fearful childhood nights, repeating my prayers in the superstitious order that Carolina had taught me. Now I wondered if Carolina had felt this panic and anxiety, too; perhaps she had invented her superstitions—encouraged by the Catholic church with its repetitive litany—to ward off these uneasy feelings. I had recently learned that my father suffered from anxiety attacks—they seemed to be a family trait.

What were we all afraid of? I wondered. Of death? Of life? As a child, I had lain in bed and worried about things like my mother dying. Over and over, I would count the years I estimated she had left to live. I feared losing her. Without her protection, life would be a dark and empty place.

Now my own life seemed to be on the line; I was counting my own years and feeling very fragile. Mothers like myself were supposed to be strong; instead, I seemed to be reliving that fearful childhood again. At night, I worried about my children. How could I help them grow if I were so disabled? Along with the ennui, panic, headaches, and insomnia, I felt ever more fragmented in the roles of wife, mother, daughter, and career woman that I was trying desperately to maintain. Where did I belong? Women of my generation wanted to be everything to everyone—to achieve, yet to nurture; to think freely, yet to honor one's parents; to be a wife, yet to be independent. These pressures seemed enormous. In more hopeful moments, I knew I was going through a transformation. But most of the time I felt hopelessly lost.

The anxiety continued as I went to doctors who prescribed medications and talked about genetic disorders, to therapists, meditation classes, and physical therapy. I wondered if a session with a Sicilian healer wouldn't cure me. But this was America; the peasant healers had long since disappeared. For me, leaping on the bandwagon of pop therapy was not appealing, although the town where I lived offered ample opportunities: Sufi dancing, Tibetan meditation, Bach flower remedies, t'ai chi. But these therapies did not spring organically out of the American tradition, culture, or land; they seemed to me to be transported or borrowed—attempts at easy solutions. Women's groups were slightly more helpful, but goddess rituals in suburban America seemed incongruous. Where was the tradition passed down through generations that would sustain them and make them real? I knew how important the rituals I had seen in Sicily were. Now these rites, a part of my religious and cultural heritage, seemed crucial to my health.

Carlo's invitation to come back to Trapani and Clara's certainty that I would return nagged at me. Giuseppe and Carlo sent letters, postcards, and pictures of the Madonna. I studied Italian and read Verga, Pirandello, and Lampedusa. Continuing to research Demeter and Persephone, I discovered other archaeological sites connected to these deities. I even became obsessed with Sicilian cuisine, cooking couscous with the semolina that Lucia had given me.

I also began to write about my debilitating experiences; this writing and the process of nurturing my roots sustained me. Finally, nearly two years later, I felt stronger, and I planned another trip to Sicily at Eastertime. Tom, who supported my quest, could not accompany me this time, and I decided to go alone. I would continue my study of Demeter and Persephone and try again to meet and talk with Sicilian women. But mostly I was returning for the procession.

When I arrived at Palermo almost three weeks before Easter, I took a bus into town to the Hotel Liguria, were I had stayed the first time I had come to Sicily with Tom. The same *signora* was there, her hair a little grayer; she remembered me and showed me to the very same room. Then I phoned Gian Carlo, hoping to find him in Palermo. He answered, surprised to hear my voice, and said he had received the telegram I had hastily sent. But he still couldn't believe that I was back.

A few hours later we sat talking in a nearby restaurant. Gian Carlo, too, had a few more gray streaks in his hair; otherwise, he had changed little. He was excited about my plans to research Demeter and Persephone further, then to see the procession again. I told him that first I wanted to go to Trapani to see my friends there, possibly staying for a few days. He suggested we meet later in the week for dinner at I Trabanesi on a day when he had appointments in Trapani. I agreed happily, knowing that this would also allow me to see Clara again.

The next day I caught an express bus to Trapani; when it arrived in the late afternoon, I got off with my bags and walked toward the Church of the Purgatory. Carlo Misterioso was standing in front, as if time had stood still. He was even wearing the same black leather jacket, two-toned thin-soled shoes, and flashy gold medallion. As if I, too, had never left, he embraced me cordially, then took my bags. He was pleased that I had returned.

Offhandedly, he then asked the inevitable question: "You are here alone?"

I found myself explaining about last-minute decisions, Tom's work preventing him from coming, articles I wanted to write. It was all very vague, and I changed the subject.

"Where are Giuseppe, Carlo . . . how is everyone?"

He looked at his watch. "Giuseppe should be finishing right now." We set off down the street toward the typography shop where Giuseppe worked.

As I stood in the shop's doorway, I could see Giuseppe in his printer's apron, standing over a printing press. "Pepe," said Carlo, "look who's here." Giuseppe glanced up, did a double take, then came to the door. Ever sentimental, he had tears in his eyes.

"Tommaso, is he here, too?"

"No, I've come alone."

He wiped his ink-stained hands on his apron, then hugged me, but I sensed a distance, as if new rules of propriety existed between us because I had arrived unchaperoned.

The final surprise was the news about Carlo Sugameli. Carlo and Giuseppe walked me to the Church of the Purgatory, inside which a pre–Holy Week display of the *Misteri* had been set up. I was standing at the foot of the *Madonna Addolorata* when Patrizia Amoroso, Giuseppe's eighteen-year-old niece, came up and announced excitedly that Carlo was engaged to be married. And I had thought that Carlo was a confirmed bachelor!

"Come, we may find Carlo at the San Francesco Church," said Patrizia. Apparently there was a devotion going on there to the *Madonna dei Massari*, a Byzantine-like painting of the Madonna. She took my arm and led me out the Purgatory's door with Giuseppe following.

Two years before, Patrizia had been one of the young girls walking with Sky and the *Ceto Ecce Homo* in the procession. Now on the way to the church, she told me of her own recent engagement and showed me a photograph of her fiancé, a Trapanese who would soon be going to a military academy in Rome.

Like the others, Patrizia expressed concern that I was in Trapani alone.

"Susanna, you must stay with my family."

I shrugged my shoulders, not knowing what to say. I knew it would be difficult to decline such an offer, though I preferred the independence of the Pensione Messina. Still, although staying with a Trapani family would jeopardize my privacy, I knew it also offered a unique opportunity. I would at last be able to experience, firsthand, the Sicilian family.

A band was starting to play outside the church, and I heard the familiar strains of my favorite procession song, *"Povero Fiore."* Carriers whom I recognized came up, thrilled to see me back. Then I spotted Lucia, who ran over, her mouth open in disbelief. She introduced me to Maria, Carlo's fiancée, who clung to her arm, already like a daughter. We stood savoring our reunion and listening to the band. Ten minutes later, Carlo arrived with a huge grin on his face. His embrace was reserved but heartfelt. Where was Tommaso? Had I really come by myself? I droned out my excuses; clearly I was an oddity and slightly suspect for having traveled to Trapani alone.

The devotion ended, and both Patrizia and Giuseppe, with Carlo intervening and saying Giuseppe's house "is your house, too," extended again the offer of a place to stay. Not daring to offend, I acquiesced. Then Carlo went off to dinner at Maria's house—food, as usual, took precedence over everything in Trapani—and I went home with Patrizia.

I spent the next three days with the Amoroso family. Giuseppe's sister, Angela, lived alone in the apartment with three children while her husband was away for six-month periods working on an oil ship in the eastern Mediterranean. That first night, Giuseppe himself arrived with his mother, Nina, whom I'd met two years before. I realized only now that Giuseppe and Nina, probably because of space limitations, lived in a separate apartment, down the street from Angela's. It was good to see Nina again. She was a short, round-faced woman of sixty-five with a cherubic expression and a turned-up nose. She still wore a simple black skirt and sweater, continuing to mourn the premature death of Giuseppe's father thirty-five years earlier.

My trip from the States had been long and exhausting, and it felt good now to be in a family setting, nurtured by the Amorosos' warmth. I was filled with sensations of well-being, like those I had experienced in Sicily before. My panicky feelings had disappeared. Retaining an almost morbidly Italian trait, I had always gauged my well-being by how a place or person made me feel about death. Some people or locations caused me unexplained anxiety. So I asked myself: Could I die in this or that location or with such and such person and feel at peace? In this Sicilian family I felt safe; I was in good hands. I laughed to myself, fantasizing that my funeral dirge would be *"Povero Fiore."*

The women bustled about as I dug into the long-missed Sicilian bread and gorged on Sicilian tuna, a delicacy. Then followed spaghetti, chicken, local wine, and, at the end of the meal, a special cake. I sat at the head of the table, a celebrity who had returned to Sicily with news to tell—of Tommaso, my mother, the boys. Everyone listened attentively; Angela's children were almost too-perfect models of good behavior, eating everything quietly and obeying Angela's commands to get things from the kitchen. I thought of my own two children, talking nonstop at the table, too excited to eat. I watched Angela's children respond to the warmth of their Uncle Giuseppe: delicious kisses, warm embraces, giggles. Some American families I knew sat in front of television sets, eating potluck style. Others ate on the run or not at all. Now, three hours from the meal's beginning, we still lingered over coffee. Finally it grew late, and Nina and Giuseppe reluctantly took their leave.

The Amorosos' apartment was small, yet Patrizia was intent on giving me her bedroom just off a small parlor with filmy curtains and gold brocade wallpaper. Patrizia, old enough to be married, wasn't a girl anymore, but her room was decorated "American style" with the pink fluff and dolls of much younger teenage girls. The dolls were everywhere: stuffed teddies, carnival dolls, little plastic Barbies. I wondered where she had got them all. My female relatives in Terracina, as well as Grandmother and Aunt Amelia, had had the same taste. Did all Italian women love this make-believe world of dolls, gauzy curtains, knickknacks, and costume jewelry? Patrizia, her sisters, and I even *became* dolls as, at Patrizia's urging, we donned pink velour pajamas embroidered with *"primo amore"* across the chest. The pair that Patrizia gave to me was new, purchased in New Town's market. All four of us sat on the bed, admiring the room's souvenirs as Patrizia recounted the history of each one; then we ogled Patrizia's engagement ring once more. The intimacy of our girls' group was fascinating and moving. I was at a maiden's slumber party, and looking down on us from the wall was a picture of a girl's version of the Virgin, complete with a Kewpie-doll face.

I guessed that these young girls, protected from the outside world, didn't know about death or dark Madonnas. The myth of Persephone's descent would have been foreign to them. But I wondered what would happen when they married, shared husbands with mistresses, lost children or parents, cooked millions of meals, and made an equal number of trips to the market. With mothers who rarely expressed their own feelings, would these girls realize how restricted their lives were? Having women like me around didn't help. Still, caught up in the world of maidenhood as they were, they couldn't conceive of or want for one moment the life they thought I had.

"Don't you miss your husband?" they asked. "How can you leave your children?" I didn't know what to say.

In some ways I envied them. Their lives were simpler, their heads uncluttered with longings, rebellions, dissatisfactions. I doubted if they had panic attacks. And they had each other: to plan weddings, cook meals, mourn deaths, sew, shop, gossip, pray, and slumber together. This solidarity was comfortable and full of magic, even if it meant a life lived separate from men.

A harem—I realized that's where I was. I saw Giuseppe only twice during the next three days, and Carlo came over just once. How different this experience was from my last visit to Trapani: the late-night dinners in restaurants, socializing with the *portatori*; the trip to Marsala with Carlo. And this harem was an unpredictable place, I learned. While these women cooked and planned their nuptials, they mocked their bridegrooms with abandon.

"Susanna, you must learn some Sicilian songs," said Patrizia. It was the third day, after *la cena*, as I sat with Angela, Patrizia and her younger sister, and Nina. We had had several cups of coffee, and Angela had even opened a

bottle of cognac. I beamed at the offer of songs and got out
my notepad.

Angela started singing. The melody and words were
similar to a song I had heard my grandmother and aunt
sing; it was about getting drunk on *"una bottiglia di vino"*
and went to a tune similar to *"Cielito Lindo."* Then the
women launched into a much racier song, consisting of
verses sung by a wife about a husband and the delicious
"banana" he was endowed with:

> *A banana chi è a frutte chiù bedda*
> *Chi impazziri li fimmini fa*
> *Si rivota tra i cosi beddi*
> *Chi ammucciati tinia u papà.*

As they sang, the women laughed and winked at one another, as if wondering whether I understood the words.
The verses continued:

> *A banana chi è a frutta chiù duci*
> *Chi impazziri li fimmini fa*
> *E magari cu un poco limuni ci mitti na brizza*
> *Torna tisu.*

The song got even more ribald, culminating in the chorus's call to women of *"Fimmini! Fimmini! Fimmini!"* Old
Nina joined in, dancing around and howling with laughter; in her black clothes she was an incongruous figure.
Patrizia grabbed my notepad, insisting she write down the
words in their Sicilian dialect. I was astonished. How could
ladies fond of dolls and Blessed Virgins be so bold? Was
this what they really did inside? What was most surprising
was that within this display of their sexuality, I detected a
tone of derision directed at their men. I was reminded of
Carolina's off-color songs and jokes, though she had no female relations, as these women did, to share them with:

calling Antonio a *caprone,* or goat, while making suggestive cuckold-horn gestures behind his back. Or her practical jokes: how when preparing food, if she accidentally dropped a tomato or piece of cheese on the kitchen floor, she would chuckle and put it on Antonio's plate. Or how she would make him "surprise" sandwiches that he would take with him to the Hackettstown railroad yard where he worked, only to find that the long loaf contained lumpy leftovers from the night before. Like Carolina, these women showed a hidden darkness when they were merry. The targets were always their husbands, whom they seemed to view as boys; the real boys, the sons, were beyond reproach.

In this apartment, dark humor was the order of the day. Angela and Nina poured another round of cognac and plunged into another song, this one a bawdy story about a cuckolded husband. I was just thinking that the singing would go on all afternoon when Patrizia looked at the clock and reminded her mother that she needed to shop for dinner. Angela put the cognac away, and Patrizia, inviting me along, went to change into a modest skirt. She called me in and suggested I wear one of her cashmere sweaters; as with the pajamas, refusal was unthinkable.

I put it on and we left the apartment—finally I was getting out. On our way to the Corso, I felt like a child walking with my mother, as Patrizia, chatting gaily, took my arm and steered me along. Now I was a proper *siciliana* going to market. We stopped at stores, buying spaghetti at one, wine at another. We bought vegetables at the outdoor market; then Patrizia remembered that she wanted some sunglasses, and she examined countless pairs at different stalls. Walking to the main street, we passed several clothing stores and stopped at a small shop where Patrizia priced a handsome two-piece suit. She said she needed something to wear to a friend's upcoming wedding. She also looked through the sparse yet elegant racks—so different from the jam-packed stores in America—at outfits she was considering for her own trousseau. I was surprised at the prices; some of the suits were $400, a lot for Angela to pay out of her husband's salary. But I had seen other girls from similar families in these outfits of silk or fine wool: a girl's wedding was the highlight of her life; for it, no holds were barred.

On the way back, Patrizia suggested we visit the *Madonna dei Trapani,* Trapani's patroness housed in the Church of the Annunciation on Via Osorio. When we arrived, a girl about Patrizia's age, dressed in full wedding regalia, posed in front of the Madonna as a professional photographer clicked away. I remembered my own wedding photos, when I had gone to a photographer's studio and stood in front of flower-painted murals. Here in Trapani, according to Patrizia, girls wanted to be photographed with this Madonna.

Like the statue in Enna, this was a virginal Madonna carved of white marble in the nineteenth century. She had an almost seductive smile on her face as she held a Christ child in her arms. Because she was a miracle worker, she was as revered in Trapani as the *Madonna Addolorata.* Everyone knew the legends about her: how the original *Madonna dei Trapani,* a statue carved of ebony, had been found in the twelfth century by some Trapani fishermen, mysteriously washed up from the sea; how a church had been built in which to venerate the statue, on the place where the Church of the Annunciation now stood; how she had soon begun to work miracles; and then how the statue had mysteriously disappeared and a new version, the statue I now saw, had been put in its place. It was a familiar story. Throughout the Mediterranean, many dark, miracle-working statues of Madonnas had appeared— often from the sea—under intriguing conditions. Most had arrived during the time of the Crusades when there was travel between the Levant and Europe. Some anthropolo-

The Madonna of Trapani; Church of the Annunciation.

gists had tracked a "Black Madonna trail" through southern Europe that corresponded with the regions once oc-
cupied by the legions of imperial Rome or with old
tin-portage routes. Many of the original Black Madonnas
remained: the Madonna of Montesserat, Spain, or the
Black Madonna of Tindari, on Sicily's northern coast,
which I hoped to visit. But others had simply vanished or
been replaced by their Caucasian counterparts.

I watched the bride in her white dress of cascading satin
and tulle. She pirouetted, then fondly touched the
Madonna's hard marble robe. I tried to imagine this girl
posed with a Black Madonna or even with *L'Addolorata*. It
was an impossible image. Yet it was ironic, for in the
East—in Japan or Tibet—white was the color of death.

Patrizia said a quick prayer to the Madonna, then
walked back along the Corso. My hand was still tucked under her arm. We stopped in yet another church along the
way, this one empty and under reconstruction.

"Susanna," she said as we blessed ourselves with holy
water, "you seem like a sister to me." She squeezed my
arm tighter as we headed back outside.

"Yes, we are sisters," I answered tentatively.

I enjoyed the warmth between us, but as we reached Old
Town and climbed the stairs to her apartment, I knew I was
beginning to feel trapped. I marveled at the role I was playing with the Amorosos, talking about weddings and cooking. I really wanted to be off seeing more of Sicily and
continuing my search for Demeter and Persephone. I was
eager to meet with Gian Carlo and talk with Clara, the
mention of whom I thought would upset Patrizia's family.
They wanted me to themselves. I was elated that they had
welcomed me back; it was more than I had expected. And
I had found the sense of family I had been looking for—the
closeness, the laughter, the food . . . In fact, for them,
life was one long dinner. But the problem was, I didn't
want to prepare it.

That night we ate a quiet meal. Giuseppe was gone, eating in a restaurant with his team of porters, making plans for the procession. After dinner I broached the subject of leaving Trapani for a few days and explained that, for my "research," I needed to explore some other places on the island.

Angela frowned. "Stay with us. In two days is another devotion to the Madonna. And the procession is next week!"

"But I'll be back by then . . ."

Patrizia hardly heard me. "And you can follow the procession with the Madonna's *ceto*," she interjected.

I looked at Patrizia, surprised at this offer. Here was a real invitation to join the procession. I pictured myself walking with the old women and mothers as they mourned people they had lost to death. It could work; after all, I had considered it two years before. I thought of a good friend who had recently died in Oregon; this time I even had a reason to follow.

"But I have no black clothes," I said, half in jest.

Patrizia motioned to the closet. "We can find you something." She grinned as if she, too, saw the humor in the situation. But she was also serious. "Please," she said, "walk with the Madonna."

"It would be an honor. But let me think about it," I replied.

I went to bed, mulling over the offer. Did I really want to identify with grieving women? Yet this might be my only chance to participate in the procession.

The next morning I told Angela and Patrizia about my dinner with Gian Carlo, scheduled for that night. They seemed hurt, then said that today was Giuseppe's birthday and they had planned a special celebration. This was awful—I wished that I had known—but I assured Angela that I wouldn't have to miss the party, since I was meeting

Church statuary and mosaic; Trapani.

Gian Carlo at 10:00 P.M. Her face showed surprise at the news of this late hour.

Then I announced that I was going out alone that morning to get some maps at the tourist office and to check on bus schedules and car rentals. Now doubly dejected, Angela said nothing and went into the kitchen. I hurried to my room to dress.

Patrizia followed, watching as I searched through my bag. I wanted to wear jeans, but she rummaged through her closet, bringing down a pile of skirts and sweaters. She was intent on outfitting me again; as before, it was difficult to refuse. We compromised: I wore my jeans and one of her sweaters. Then she got out a jewelry box and held up a gold necklace.

"This will look beautiful on you."

"Oh, no, it's too nice."

"It's perfect. Come on!" She laughed, then pretended to be angry. "I insist."

I put on the necklace. She was still fishing through the box; finally she found what she was looking for and told me to put out my hand. I saw that she was holding a wedding band.

For years I hadn't worn my wedding ring because it was too tight. But I hadn't thought about what its absence might mean to Sicilians, who were always careful to define a woman's status, marital or otherwise.

Patrizia looked despairingly at my empty finger.

"You should wear it."

It was an awkward moment. To refuse would seem, to Patrizia, a denial of my marriage. I slipped it on and found that it fit. Patrizia now thought me acceptable: I was ready to face the town's judging eyes. I went into the kitchen to say good-bye to Angela, then walked down to the street.

In Patrizia's clothes and accessories, I felt like Doris Day or Debbie Reynolds, off to some tea or an afternoon of shopping. This playacting was alarming. I was not only seeing the harem from the inside but, like a method actor, I was actually trying it on for size.

I picked up the maps at the tourist office, then went to the bus station to plan an itinerary that would take me around the island. I wanted to leave tomorrow, going south along the coast and stopping at Selinunte and Agrigento, where there were sanctuaries dedicated to Demeter. I was discouraged to discover that the bus trip to Selinunte, only 150 miles away, would take five hours. I spent an hour looking for a car rental agency only to find that it was closed. It was midday and everyone was at *la cena*.

Not wanting to return to the Amorosos' so soon, I took a long walk along Trapani's seafront. Out by the Torre de Ligny, a tower dating from the twelfth-century Norman occupation, I walked among immense orange and blue fishing nets stretched out to dry. Not even the fishermen were about; the town appeared to be all mine. A sharp wind was blowing, as it always did on Trapani's unprotected Tyrrhenian seaside. I put Patrizia's necklace underneath the sweater and ran along the causeway toward the tower and Trapani's very tip.

Climbing onto the rock at the tower's base, then shimmying along a narrow ledge, I sat huddled against the howling wind. Here, where few came except lovers or young boys to fish, I faced toward Africa, with Levanzo, where the cave goddess was, before me. Looking south, I could see the Sicilian coastline; ominous bluish cliffs, rising through the haze, looked like the scales on some sea monster's back. Selinunte and Agrigento, then Syracuse stretched far to the southeast. In these places Demeter and Persephone had been worshiped, in their temples and sanctuaries. Would I find traces of them now? Or were they trapped—like me during this stay in Trapani—somewhere in my imagination?

I left my lookout and headed back along the causeway.

The stores were open now, and I stopped in one to buy a present for Giuseppe, an expensive bottle of liquor. When I got back to the Amorosos', Nina, Patrizia, and Angela were busy in the kitchen preparing the birthday dinner. I retreated to the bedroom to pack for the next day's departure.

Giuseppe arrived about 7:00 and I went out to greet him; he, too, was upset that I was leaving, even with my promises to return in a week. I had heard Angela tell him about my dinner with Gian Carlo. Although he said nothing about it to me, he seemed distant. Was I imagining things, or had I upset the entire household by the plans I had made? To lighten the mood, I gave Giuseppe his present, which included a card I had made. He looked thoughtfully at my Italian words of affection and was impressed with the expensive liquor.

"Open it," I urged.

"No, no." He waved his arms and put it on a knickknack shelf. He wanted to save it.

Our dinner was unusually quiet, especially for a birthday celebration. I wanted to eat sparingly, considering the coming meal with Gian Carlo, but it was impossible. Angela loaded the table with tuna, chicken, *carne arrosto*, spaghetti, and delicious greens drenched in oil and garlic. Obeying Nina's intermittent commands of *mangia*, I ate. No one talked; the only sounds were our clattering forks and the clock, which Patrizia looked at occasionally as it ticked ominously in the background. All of a sudden, as if to break the ice, Giuseppe put a video in the VCR that he had borrowed for the night. I was amazed at this display of Americanness. The video was a Sicilian television documentary about the annual *mattanza*, a traditional spearing of tuna off Favignana Island near Trapani every June. I stared at muscled fishermen spearing hundreds of tuna, which they had funneled into a series of net chambers, a technique dating from the Arab occupation. The

fishermen droned an Arab chant as the spears flew, turning the death chamber a bilious red. Watching the bloody
thrashing, I took a look at the meat on my plate and could
eat no more.

Everyone's eyes were fixed on the last tuna left in the
net, swimming madly for freedom. Giuseppe put down his
fork, glanced at me, then back to the video.

"*Il Cristo*," he said solemnly, pointing to the lone tuna,
then picked up his fork and resumed eating.

It was 9:30 before Giuseppe's cake was served and, with
it, cognac; Nina cut me a big piece, although I had asked
for something small. I started making excuses about
having to leave soon, mentioning the time; everyone
exchanged glances with each other but said nothing. Exasperated, I tried to make conversation. It seemed an eter-
nity before Giuseppe finished his cake. Now it was all right
for me to depart.

"I'm sorry, I must go," I blurted out, trying to sound casual. I got up from the table.

"Oh, it's so late!" said Nina, yawning.

Giuseppe looked at me forlornly.

I went over to him. "And *buon' compleanno*, Giuseppe—
happy birthday." I kissed him and Nina on both cheeks,
smiled at everyone else, then walked quietly into Patrizia's
room to get my coat. In the dining room, it was quiet
enough to hear a pin drop.

"*Buona notte*," I called as I walked to the front door.

"*Buona notte*," responded Angela. Again there was silence from the dining room. As my hand grasped the door
handle, her voice rang out again abruptly. "Don't forget to
ring the buzzer when you get back," she called, with a last
Parthian shot. "We will have to let you in."

I ran down to the Pensione Messina where Gian Carlo
and I had arranged to meet. It was already after 10:00, and
I was afraid that I had missed him. I breathed a sigh of relief

at the sight of him, trench coat fluttering in the wind, standing by his car outside the hotel.

"What in the world have you been doing?" he asked. "Where have you been staying?"

It was like reporting to my dad or an older brother. Words flooded out describing my experiences with the Amorosos' while Gian Carlo, listening with a therapist's concentration, maneuvered the car through the narrow streets. He chuckled when I told him of the Amorosos' protectiveness and how hard it had been to orchestrate our meeting.

He looked over with a grin. "Now you know how difficult life is for the women here."

But there was something too glib about his response, and it upset me. Did he really understand? Probably, in theory, but in practice, he could never really experience the life of a Sicilian woman. Nor could he know how difficult it was for me, as an American woman, to be "trying on" that life. This experiment had seemed much easier in theory than it was proving to be in practice.

We arrived at the restaurant, which was filled with a fair crowd of late-night diners. Clara, standing by a table of customers, saw us and came over. She embraced me, then grinned; I was amazed at how matter-of-fact she seemed at my return.

"I knew you would come back," she said.

She found us a table, then returned to her other customers. Gian Carlo ordered several courses, but I begged off; Giuseppe's dinner and the images of dead tuna had destroyed my appetite. I watched the diners and followed Clara as she circulated among them. I was intrigued by her demeanor, so unlike that of other Sicilian women I had seen preparing food or presiding over tables. She was stately and detached; moving slowly, she drifted from table to table greeting customers or serving food. She reminded me of a countess inspecting her garden or, when she put on her glasses to read a menu, of an eccentric professor about to give a lecture.

Through the entire meal, she didn't once come over to our table. I was disappointed, as now the restaurant's crowd had thinned. Was she avoiding me? I hoped she hadn't forgotten our conversation and the offer she had made two years before.

By midnight the restaurant was almost empty; Gian Carlo was finishing a dessert as I talked about my plans for touring the island. I wondered whether he or even Clara might like to come along, at least as far as Agrigento. But he said he had a busy work schedule before Easter and was sure that Clara did, too. I was disappointed; although I knew that this was an eleventh-hour request and that I should make the journey alone, I was beginning to feel a little leery about my plans. A sympathetic Sicilian would have been a welcome companion.

Clara, after resetting the empty tables, finally sat down with us. She took off her glasses, then looked squarely at me.

"And you, Susanna—what are you going to do in Trapani this time?"

"I'm going to travel for a while, then I want to come back for the procession again."

I told her a little about the experiences with the Amorosos' and their invitation to walk in the procession with the Madonna.

Clara peered at me. For a moment, she was quiet.

"And will you do this?" she asked.

"I don't know . . ."

"But don't you remember what I said to you before?"

"Oh, yes."

"You must come with me. We can go out into the night together."

I was overjoyed: she hadn't forgotten. With this invitation, I would be able to walk with her as she carried the *Ceto*

Salinai. This is where I felt I belonged, with an independent woman of action rather than with passive women dressed in black. Clara also suggested that I visit her at her apartment when I got back from my trip. Could I come the following Wednesday? She would have the day off, and we could talk some more. She gave me her address, then said good night and went into the kitchen to lock up.

It was 1:00 A.M. by the time Gian Carlo and I left the restaurant. I was exhausted and worried about getting back into the Amorosos' apartment. Gian Carlo sped through the deserted streets and pulled up to the building, then waited as I got out and pressed the apartment buzzer. After a long pause, it buzzed back, and I waved to him.

"See you when you get back. Good luck!" he said.

I felt abandoned. Gian Carlo was my sounding board, an interpreter of my Sicilian experiences. Now I would be on my own, not seeing him until Good Friday when he would come back to Trapani for the procession. I opened the street door and went inside, trudging up the four floors in the darkness to the apartment of women who waited for me above.

It was Patrizia who had buzzed me in. She stood in her pajamas in the doorway of her mother's bedroom where she had been sleeping.

"Shhh . . . everyone's asleep!" She held her finger to her lips, then turned on a small lamp so I could see. I felt guilty, like a high school girl returning home long past my curfew. How often I had had this experience in the past. Sometimes Mother had waited up for me, but usually it had been Dad, worried and angry and convinced that a daughter out past midnight was surely asking for, if not already in, trouble. I felt guilty, too, at betraying Patrizia and Angela by my decision to join Clara in the procession. On that night I would certainly be out late. In fact, I probably would not come "home" at all.

I whispered good night to Patrizia, closed the door to the

room, took off my clothes, and collapsed on the bed. Although I was tired, I couldn't sleep. I felt confused and a little panicky about leaving; why couldn't I just stay right here in the Amorosos' protective cocoon? I remembered one of my grandmother's Italian proverbs: "Your mother's house is warm, is safe, is gold. Outside is dark, is black; the wolf is there."

At about 3:00 A.M. I finally fell asleep, just as the neighborhood roosters began to crow. The alarm rang at 9:00 A.M.; I forced myself up and gathered my bags together. Hurrying out, I quickly said good-bye to Angela and Patrizia, and closed the door behind me. I was off—to what I was not sure. At the top of the stairs, Angela, a look of bewilderment on her face, stood watching me go. What kind of woman was I? she seemed to wonder. I remembered another Italian proverb, which made me feel strangely sexless and alone: "The woman at the window, the man on the road."

But even the "road" was in question, as I shortly discovered. At the rental agency there were cars available and the cost was reasonable. But in a colossal oversight, I had left my driver's license in the States, and the agent would not rent me a car without it. I was furious, realizing that I would have to go by bus after all; my journey around Sicily would take twice as long. Plus, I had already missed the bus to Agrigento. But the agent, Salvo, had an idea. He had a friend who worked at Trapani's airport and was driving to Syracuse in a few hours. Could I change my itinerary a bit? Yes, of course I could, I said. Salvo called him and set everything up. He drove me out to the airport, and while we waited for Paolo, we loaded my bags into his car.

The dark-eyed Paolo, a thirty-year-old mechanic, soon appeared. We got in; he put on a set of radio headphones, roared out of the airport parking lot, and sped onto the freeway toward Palermo. In an hour we had passed the city and turned inland. I looked at my driver, now wearing wraparound sunglasses and engrossed in his music. Was I with one of my grandmother's wolves? I didn't care. I adjusted the seat so that I could lie back, and as we cut steadily across the island toward Syracuse, I soon fell asleep.

CHAPTER VII

Syracuse Revisited

ALL THAT I COULD see of the once-great Greek city of Syracuse when we arrived in the dark were the torchlike towers of the oil refineries of adjoining Agusta, blazing red in the blackened sky. Paolo, whose parents lived on the other side of Syracuse, went an hour out of his way to drive me to Ortigia where I wanted to stay, a small island linked to the city by a bridge.

He parked on Via Savoia, and I found a room in the hotel just across the street. It was expensive, but it was too late to search for bargains. Back at the car, I got my bags and thanked Paolo; he had been a friendly escort, after all, and we had made Syracuse in record time.

I ate a late meal in the hotel's restaurant and pored over maps of Syracuse. On my first visit to Sicily, I had come here after Easter for a few days and had seen some of its great sites. The most renowned was the Greek theater, built in 500 B.C., where the plays of Aeschylus were performed. This immense limestone amphitheater, with seats cut into the hillside, was considered by some to be the Mediterranean's most important Greek ruin. I had also visited the Latomie, the stone quarries where seven thousand survivors of the Athenian army, whose fleet had been defeated in Syracuse's harbor in 413 B.C., had been kept prisoner. There had been a strong sense of death in the cool stone walls and the huge abyss below, which was like an open-pit mine now overgrown with bougainvillea. I had imagined the prisoners crowded into one portion of it for eight months, their daily allowance, according to Thucydides, half a pint of water and a pint of corn. Most had died or been sold as slaves, symbols of the long history of Syracuse's tyrannical rule over Sicily under Gelon, Hieron, and Dionysius the Elder.

It was hard to like Syracuse. I felt a coldness in this city of unruly traffic and oversized crumbling monuments. Unlike the people of western Sicily or even Palermo, the Syracusans seemed unfriendly and confused about their past. The fifth century B.C. Temple of Athena on Ortigia, now transformed into a Catholic church, summed up this confusion. Intrigued, I had studied the temple's towering Doric columns that supported a baroque facade where a gold shield of the goddess, Athena, had once been. From the sides of the church, more of these somber Doric columns protruded, still providing the church's structure, with Gothic masonry in between. The church testified to the synthesis of Christian and pagan. But instead of Athena, a statue of Syracuse's patron saint, the virgin martyr Saint Lucia, now stood triumphant on the church's facade.

Still, the old goddesses weren't entirely missing from Syracuse. In nearby Palazzolo Acreide, a former Greek colony, important 300 B.C. bas-reliefs of Demeter had been found. And at the Fonte Ciane, a pool at the source of the Ciane River, which fed into Syracuse's big port, dwelled the fabled nymph Ciane, who was associated with the myth of Demeter and Persephone. It was to Palazzolo and the fountain that I would head the next day.

The next morning I discovered that these destinations were difficult to reach. I walked to Ortigia's little harbor and talked with a fisherman who boated tourists across the port and up the Ciane River to the fountain. He said he would take me but for a round-trip charge of $50. I declined, surprised at the high fee, and walked on. Looking at my map, I decided first to take a bus inland fifteen miles to Palazzolo. Afterward, on the way back, I would get off at a stop that seemed to be about two miles from the fountain's source. If Demeter had walked all around Sicily while searching for Persephone, surely I could make this short hike myself.

I stored my bags at the hotel desk, thinking that I might change to a less expensive hotel when I returned. The bus station was a long walk across Ortigia's bridge, but I was soon riding up the agave-covered hill, above Syracuse, toward Palazzolo.

Few people had heard about the *Santoni*, or bas-reliefs of Demeter, at Palazzolo. When I asked the bus driver about them, he looked at me quizzically. Who was this Demeter, and why wasn't I interested in Palazzolo's fine Greek theater or in the Latomie? I found myself describing the myth of Demeter and Persephone to him. Why had these important deities, once known throughout the island, been forgotten? I began to find out when I arrived in Palazzolo and hiked another five hundred feet above the village, on a winding road, to the ruin's entrance to the amphitheater. I was the only visitor, and two gatekeepers were eager to show me inside.

"No, *grazie*, I want to see the *Santoni*."

"But, *signora*, the theater is very beautiful," said one.

"No," I persisted. "I only have a little time. I want to see the images of Demeter, in the rock. *Dov'e sono?* Where are they?"

The gatekeepers glanced at each other. One sighed, then went into the ticket office, returned with a key, and motioned toward a small car parked nearby. We drove back down the road to a point a hundred feet below the back side of the ruins. We climbed out, and the man toyed with the locked gate; from the look of the rusted chain, it seemed that few people came here. Inside the gate, a narrow path led into a steep ravine. To my right, up against a rock wall, were four odd-looking little wooden houses. At first, I thought they were tool or storage sheds. Then the gatekeeper opened one of them. Inside it was a six-foot-high rock sculpture of Demeter: one of the *Santoni.* How like this deity, I thought, to be hidden in such a remote place. No wonder the Sicilians knew so little about her.

The man opened the other doors: each of them held a magnificent bas-relief of Demeter, sitting as if on a throne and carved skillfully into the living rock. Sadly, in all of them her face had badly eroded. In one, a small child, Persephone, had been carved at Demeter's side. I went up close to look, standing almost inside the little doors, and could smell the darkness around me. A nest of beetles on the dirt floor, their backs an iridescent purple, scurried out of the way. Then I looked up, startled to see a small snake creeping up Persephone's form. Black against the white stone, it spiraled across her chest and almost curled back on itself. I was surprised, yet thought of the appropriateness of this traditional symbol of fertility. It formed a uroborus—the image of a snake feeding on its own tail. I remembered that Persephone's Latin name was Proserpina. Besides being a "savior," she was also known as First Serpent.

This ravine below the ruins seemed to be a pre-Christian sanctuary, a place of the dead. Sicily's chthonic sanctuaries were almost always associated with Demeter and Persephone, and ancients believed that these openings in the ground were passageways to the kingdom of the dead. The souls of the departed, who could foresee the future, lived here, and these spirits were sometimes threatening to mor-

Like Sicily's women, Demeter spends a life inside; the Santoni, *Greek ruins, Palazzolo Acreide.*

tals. In the books I had read, I had been impressed with accounts of how women had willingly entered these sanctuaries—called *necromanteia* by the Greeks—to commemorate Queen Persephone's journey to Hades. At Eleusis or the Acheron in Greece, they had first gone into a chamber to eat foods associated with the dead: beans, barley bread, and pork. Afterward, they had been sequestered in another chamber for prayer. Then, bringing offerings of sacrificed sheep and sacred cakes made of grain and honey and formed into the shape of vulvas, which represented Persephone's return to her mother, they had entered a maze of passageways leading to the final chamber. There lived Persephone. The pilgrims had presented their offerings and made supplications to the dead souls, represented by the goddess. Perhaps in a hallucinatory state induced by the vigorous diet, they had communed with the dead, asking advice and garnering strength for their own lives. Then they had left through a different passageway, returning to the upper world and completing the serpentine path. Their visit to Proserpina had restored them. Just as the snake bites its tail, death had become life in a circle of regeneration.

The little snake that now spiraled across Persephone's chest was a sign, another link to the past I sought. I remembered, in fact, how much my grandmother had been afraid of snakes. Even a garter snake would set her running. One day Grandpa had brought home a bronze art deco candelabra in the form of a magnificent snake. It was coiled proudly upright, two humanlike "arms" holding candles. Grandma had refused to have it in her house and had given it to Mother the next time she had come to Oregon to visit. But I had been attracted to the snake, and eventually talking Mother out of it, I had brought it home, where it remained on my mantle. It held a kind of power for me; the candles held up by the snake's arms seemed to offer hope and light.

Now I lamented how much our modern attitude toward the serpent and the underground it symbolized had changed. With Christianity's story of Eve's temptation in the garden, most of us had learned to mistrust anything unknown and snakelike, and we feared the dark place — the very earth itself — in which the serpent lived. Ultimately, we feared the dark place in ourselves.

Unnecessarily, we separated life from death. Now, the old mysteries that celebrated the dead were barely a memory and Persephone and Demeter nearly unknown. I wondered how many icons and statues of the goddesses, unearthed at these sanctuaries, had been carted off to museums. Ironically, here at Palazzolo, the few remaining images of the deities were hidden away, behind closed doors, locked inside little houses. I studied the curious sheds, cleverly built around the protruding rock to protect the bas-reliefs from the weather. Still, I couldn't help but think how these locked-up deities were metaphors for Sicilian women in general and for my own experiences in Trapani.

Our time was up and the gatekeeper ceremoniously closed the four doors, one by one. Like the Madonna as she entered the church on Holy Saturday, Demeter and her daughter disappeared from view. I felt sad. Staring at doors that seldom opened, these deities were ensconced in darkness again.

I wanted to linger awhile, keeping watch over the little houses. But the gatekeeper, pronouncing it lunchtime, hurried me back up the ravine. We drove up to the ticket office; then I walked down to Palazzolo's central square. Luckily a bus was just leaving for Syracuse, and the driver agreed to drop me off at the road to the fountain. But was I *really* walking? No one ever did that. He shook his head in amazement, then started the bus.

We lumbered down the cactus-covered, rocky hillsides and were soon in a narrow green belt of citrus orchards, palm, and oleander. I was the only passenger to get off at the stop where a dilapidated sign read "Fonte Ciane." Waving at the driver and the peasant women peering out the windows of the bus, I slung my camera bag over my shoulder and started off down a country lane.

It wound through a little valley, wonderfully fragrant with the scent of orange and lemon. On both sides orchards bulged with fruit: huge lemons and the "bleeding oranges" with ruby-red centers named after Christ's blood. An occasional deserted villa appeared amid the orchards; around one bend I encountered a man in his sixties, neatly dressed and looking like a city farmer, who carefully climbed down a ladder placed next to a tree and loaded a sack of oranges into the trunk of his car. When I passed by, he held up some oranges, two to a fist, offering them to me as a gift. But where would I put them? I took off my outer shirt, tied the sleeves together, filled it with oranges, and slung it around my neck.

I ate greedily as I walked along. After an hour I hadn't seen another person and estimated I had gone at least two miles. But there was no sign of the fountain. The road meandered stubbornly through the valley; when I got to a rise, I could see that the papyrus stand that marked the fountain was still several miles away. Another hour passed and I had walked over two miles more. Still no one passed me on the road. Was this the right way? Now I understood the bus driver's skepticism and wondered if I would arrive by dark. Afterward, how would I get back to the highway and Syracuse again?

Finally I heard a motorcycle approaching, coming from the direction of the fountain. A dark-haired man in his early thirties careened by. Looking over his shoulder at me, he turned around and came back, stopping in front of me. He reminded me of photographs I had seen of Mussolini, dressed in jodhpurs and black, knee-high boots. I was as amazed to see this militaristic-looking man as he was to encounter a foreigner hiking in the heat and loaded down with a camera bag and satchel of oranges. Without a word, he sat cross-armed on the cycle.

"*Il Fonte Ciane,* do you know where it is?" I asked, wondering if I should be relieved or worried at his abrupt appearance.

"About a mile," he said, looking down the road. Then he turned back to me. "Would you like a ride?"

I thought of my trip with Roberto down the road from Enna and decided that I wasn't in the mood for a similar adventure.

"No, *grazie,*" I said and started walking again.

"But, *signorina* . . ." he persisted, scooting along behind me on the cycle.

I ignored him and continued on. He followed for a while longer, offering the ride yet again. I shook my head; he gave up and zoomed back toward the fountain.

In a half hour, I arrived at an empty parking lot. There was no sign of the motorcyclist, but beyond the lot, a path led off through a papyrus grove. No one was about; it was unusually quiet except for the sound of the wind rattling the papyrus trees. I jogged down the path through the grove, which shortly opened on a large, crystalline pool: this was, undoubtedly, the Fountain of Ciane. Hoping not to offend the nymph, I dropped my bag and the oranges, took off my shoes, and sat on a rock, dangling my feet in the cool water.

It was an apt place for legends. The bordering papyrus, brought to Syracuse by the Arabs from Egypt, cast withering shadows on the water; in the dim light, the pool seemed spookily deep. It was clean, unlike other rivers I had encountered in Sicily. Like a heart-shaped womb, the pool had its outlet in the narrow opening of the Ciane River on the other side, funneling into it as though into a vaginal canal. I thought about Ciane and the legend associated with this place. Here, on the banks of the pool, she had

encountered Demeter in her relentless search for Persephone. She had warned Demeter of the approaching Pluto; in
punishment, Pluto had frozen Ciane in the pool forever. To
me it seemed more like a reward to float eternally in these
clean waters. I looked hard into the pool, almost hoping to
see her.

I had read that brides often came here to be photographed against the backdrop of the pool, as they did at
the Church of the Annunciation in Trapani. I was relieved
that, for now, no girls in white flitted about. I set up my tripod to take a photograph, studying the rippling patterns
on the water as it lapped softly against the banks. I was just
about to release the shutter when into the viewfinder came
a boat, entering the pool from the river's outlet. The boat
was full of tourists shouting above the blaring motor and
manned by none other than the fisherman I had met earlier
in the day. He waved at me, then motored the long
wooden boat right up to where I was standing. Throwing
out a rope and jumping onto shore, he greeted me like a
long-lost friend. When I told him that I had walked, he
shook his head in disbelief. Surely I was very tired. But, he
suggested, perhaps I would like a ride back? His son was
coming in a few minutes, in another boat right behind him,
and between the two of them, they had plenty of room.
Since I would only be going halfway, he said I could have
a sizable reduction in fare.

I said yes, glad for a ride back to Syracuse. But I was disappointed at the noisy intrusion that he and his boatload
of tourists made on the fountain's serenity. In addition, my
photograph was jeopardized as the boat now bobbed right
in front of my camera. I looked through the viewfinder
again, trying to resign myself to using the boat as a frame
for the fountain. It was a handsome Sicilian fishing boat,
unusually long with fitted boards painted white. My eyes
followed the curve of the upturned prow until I came upon
a startling image. At the prow's tip was a large, cylindrical

form surging upward almost two feet, like the stylized masthead of a Manila galleon. The form was undeniably a phallus. I lifted my eyes from the lens, now noticing shorter, similar shapes along the boat's sides. Here was a dramatic meeting of male and female space—a symbolic penetration, in this womblike fountain, of the waters of Ciane.

On the side of the boat was the shape of an elongated eye, painted black. It resembled a stylized version of the Eye of Isis, seen in Egyptian hieroglyphs, which had been a symbol of the power that the Egyptian deity Isis had received from the Sun God, Ra. The eye looked like a fish, its outer corner curving around into a brow.

Isis had been worshiped in upper Egypt until the sixth century A.D. Like Demeter and Persephone, she was a goddess of fertility. After mourning the death of her husband, Osiris, she had found the "pieces" of his body—except the phallus, which she had to recreate—in the River Nile and had reassembled them. In yearly spring rituals in Egypt, Isis, symbolized by a boat, searched for Osiris, who personified the Nile and caused its yearly flooding and fertilization of the land and of her. After Rome had conquered Egypt, the cult of Isis had spread throughout the Mediterranean. She became known as the "One with Ten Thousand Names" and was identified with Demeter, Persephone, and other aspects of womanhood that were embodied in Greek deities such as Aphrodite, Artemis, and Hecate.

I watched the gently bobbing boat, now a mythic presence in the blue waters. So many connections were possible: the Ciane River was Osiris, Persephone, or even Christ, and the boat was Isis, Demeter, and the Madonna—the deities who, through their quests for lost children or husbands, made regeneration possible.

Another boat came into view and tied up next to the first. It was navigated by the first boatman's son. They talked,

Fisherman's boat; Fonte Ciane, Syracuse.

the father deciding to take the tourists back and the son agreeing to wait for me. The tourists piled into the first boat, which motored into the channel. I took some photographs and a half hour later I left the fountain with the son. Standing in the prow, I glanced back at the lonely fountain. The boat's motor hadn't started, so the only sound was the lapping of the oars. Then the abrupt roar of a motorcycle's engine cut through the air. I looked at the far shore to see the man on the motorcycle drive up to the spot where I had been standing. He screeched to a halt, and, as if he were looking for someone, scanned the fountain with his hand shading his eyes. He spotted us, then watched our disappearance into the narrow channel.

I was relieved that I hadn't encountered him again, and I lay back in the boat, watching the swaying papyrus above me. The feathery tips met, forming a bower over my head. I felt content; now I could return to a good night's sleep at the hotel.

The river, only several yards wide at some points, flowed quietly along under arching bridges; at one point, we stopped at a small lock system while a man on shore raised the water level so that we could pass. We motored on as the river widened. When we reached the bay, the fading light turned the buff-colored domes and turrets of Syracuse's skyline, across the water, a dark orange. We crossed the open water of the bay and were soon docked in Ortigia's harbor, by a piazza not far from the hotel. I climbed out of the boat, paying and thanking the boy, and arrived at the hotel just as it was getting dark.

It had not occurred to me, in this slow time before Holy Week, to worry about renting my room for a second night. But when I went to the desk, the concierge informed me that the hotel was booked. I pleaded with him in vain, but he shook his head and suggested a hotel down the street. I took my bags and hurried out. The other hotel was also full. Tired and exasperated, I headed for the piazza to consult my map. There were other hotels, but most were located in the center of Syracuse, a long walk away.

As I sat at a table jotting down directions, I heard a voice behind me.

"*Ciao, signorina* . . . Did you enjoy the fountain?"

I turned around; it was the man on the motorcycle.

His motorcycle was nowhere to be seen, and he had changed his clothes to a white shirt and a pair of dark slacks. I smiled nervously, continuing to look over my maps. He sat down and watched me.

"What are you doing?" he asked.

Abruptly, I told him of my plight and said that I was looking for a hotel room for the night.

He looked at my map.

"You can probably find another, but you will have to walk very far. And the buses have stopped running."

I put the map and notes away and started to get up.

"*Signorina* . . ." He jumped up, pulling out my chair. "I can take you to some hotels by the train station. I have a car, just over there."

I looked at the little Fiat parked by the piazza. I studied his face: he was younger than I had thought, about twenty-five. Without his jodhpurs and boots, he seemed less threatening. As at Enna, it was against my better judgment to accept a ride, but I felt desperate. There weren't any taxis around, it was almost dark, and I knew I had to find a hotel room soon.

Trying to sound businesslike, I agreed to let him take me, on the condition that I pay him for his trouble. He refused but I put some lira notes in my pocket, ready to pay him when we arrived. At his car, he opened the passenger's door for me. I peered inside, surprised to see a baby bottle and some children's toys strewn across the seat. He was unnerved by my seeing this evidence of his private life and quickly threw the bottle and toys into the back, which also contained a baby's car seat. He put my duffel bag into the backseat, then I got in with my camera bag, and he closed the door behind me.

As soon as we headed out of the plaza, I regretted my decision. Unlike Roberto in Enna, he quickly barraged me with personal questions: Was I married? Where were my husband and children? I deflected his queries, pretending not to fully understand him. Staring straight ahead, I watched for the train station, which I had seen, briefly, from the bus window that morning.

We drove down the Corso Umberto but, about halfway to the city center, he veered off onto a side street.

"Per la stazione?" I asked, warily.

"Sì, un giro lungo" — we were taking a detour to the station because of the traffic. This disturbed me, but I gave him the benefit of the doubt, since we were still paralleling the Corso. He looked over at me, curious to know why I was in Syracuse and what I had been doing at the fountain. I tried to smile and wondered what to say. Meanwhile he reached out for my hand and asked me why I wasn't wearing a wedding ring. I glared at him, pulling my hand away and thinking that Patrizia's borrowed jewelry hadn't been such a bad idea, after all.

My growing suspicions about this fellow were quickly proved right. Soon, we were in an industrial section near the city's western end. We were definitely not near the station.

"We must go back." I pointed out my window in the direction I thought the station might be.

He looked at me seductively, his eyes gleaming in the lights on the car's dashboard.

"Please, *signore*, I want to find a hotel. Turn around!"

Instead, he accelerated. Beginning to panic, I looked outside the window and suddenly saw familiar landmarks: we were turning onto the highway for Palazzolo and the exit to the fountain. My driver was obviously not another well-meaning Roberto.

"This is not the way to the station!" I shouted.

"Signorina . . ." He slowed down and reached for my hand again, trying to calm me. "Relax. We are going to Fonte Ciane." Then the car charged into the darkness as Syracuse's lights disappeared behind us.

I couldn't believe it. Ciane's fountain, to which just hours before I had made a pilgrimage, was now to be the trysting place for the carrying out of my driver's amorous intentions. The nymph had helped Demeter, but where was she now to ward off this abducting Pluto? I was apparently on my own.

Sitting forward in the seat, I clutched the door handle, and as Persephone surely must have done, I screamed at the top of my lungs: *"Immediatamente, signore!* Stop immediately!"

Perhaps this frightened him, or perhaps he had thought better of his seduction techniques. He pulled into a turnout, stopped the car, and stared at me. I was shaking, but I managed to open the car door, grab my bag from behind the seat, and throw it out onto the highway. With my camera bag, I jumped out and slammed the door. He rolled down the window, shouting "Fonte Ciane! Fonte Ciane!" as I crossed the highway and ran along the narrow shoulder toward the oncoming traffic. I looked in horror as he turned around, speeding toward me. He narrowly missed running me down, then sped off toward Syracuse.

I was trembling in disbelief at what had happened. Worse, the full impact of my situation began to sink in. I was about five miles from the center of Syracuse, it was pitch-black, and the highway was unlit, with no place where I could walk safely. Plus, I was worried that the man would return. I ran down the road toward the city, stumbling into thorn-filled gullies to hide from the motorists that occasionally passed by. I did not dare flag down a car—what if it were the returning abductor? Besides, I couldn't trust anyone to help me now.

As I continued walking, sometimes in the gully, sometimes on the minuscule shoulder, I thought miserably of my grandmother's admonition and of the "wolf" in the proverb. But when, after about two miles, the man had not returned, I began to feel safer. Now the increasing traffic demanded my full attention, as I threaded a narrow path between the speeding cars and the steep embankment. Finally, I could see the first lights of Syracuse twinkling in the distance.

As my fear subsided, I began to seethe with anger. How could this man have deceived me so? I trudged along, glaring at the passing motorists. One slowed down, its occupant a man with a swarthy complexion and beady eyes that stared back at me from the window. I motioned him on. Most of the cars' occupants only glanced at me in disbelief as they passed by, as if they were seeing an apparition. It was unbelievable for a woman to be out like this. At about 11:00 P.M., I walked off the highway where it joined a main road into Syracuse.

Half an hour later I was at the train station, out of breath and dripping with perspiration. Across the street, I could see the lights of several hotels, and I hurried over. No rooms were available in any of them. Undaunted by the third unsympathetic concierge who looked suspiciously at my appearance, I insisted he call a five-star hotel, located near the Greek theater and listed in my guidebook. He phoned. They had a room; I did not even ask the price. Then I asked him to call a taxi from the terminal, which promptly arrived.

It was the most expensive taxi ride and hotel room I had ever had in Sicily. I paid the driver $25 and plunked down $75 on the hotel's chrome-plated desk. A bellhop brought my bags up to the room on the tenth floor. It was luxurious, with a view of the Greek theater far below and the lights of the city sparkling all around. But I felt that this beauty was deceiving; after today, Syracuse had become even harder to like.

I drew a bath and stepped into the scalding water; I was scratched, torn, and exhausted. But I had made it.

CHAPTER VIII

The Black Madonna
of Tindari

THE NEXT MORNING I left Syracuse, huddled in a second-class compartment of an express train that sped up the Ionian coast. The drizzling rain outside matched my gray mood. On the almost empty train, I watched out the window as we passed lonely beach resorts and the city of Catania, eternally covered with soot from centuries of explosions of the now-shrouded Mount Etna. The coast route became mountainous with soaring cliffs on one side and long drops to the sea on the other. The train careened into an old stone tunnel, built in block construction like a Roman aqueduct, then rattled into the stop for Taormina. Seeing the picturesque resort perched a thousand feet above me on the rocky cliffs, I was momentarily tempted to get off. I could stay a few days, relaxing in one of the spectacular hotel villas overlooking the sea. Though this had been my original plan, I was now too tired to deal with hotel concierges, taxi drivers, or dubious Sicilian men. For the moment, this train was a safe haven, and I stayed steadfast in my seat.

The train left Taormina, and we wound along a still

mountainous track, past little villages above us and hot-pink bougainvillea, daphne, and wild roses spilling down the rocks. It was Palm Sunday, the first day of Holy Week. Families at stations along the way, crowded under umbrellas, carried palm fronds and gaily boxed Easter breads as they hurried to mass. Though I would have to return to Trapani soon, I was now going in the opposite direction toward the province of Messina. That morning, with a change in my itinerary, I had decided to go to Tindari up on the north coast of Sicily, instead of continuing clockwise to Agrigento. At Tindari, I planned to visit the sanctuary of the Black Madonna. I had stopped there on my last trip to Sicily when we had arrived on the island via the Straits of Messina. But I hadn't actually seen the famed statue of the Madonna; it had been late in the day and the church had been closed. Now, I felt compelled to try again. Unlike Ciane or the faceless *Santoni*, I wouldn't have to imagine her. She was real: a diminutive yet reputedly awe-inspiring Madonna with a coal-black face.

Actually finding the sanctuary again was like threading my way through a Cretan maze. At Messina, a port just five miles across the straits from the toe of Italy's boot, I took a second train that turned westward along the Tyrrhenian coast. I changed a third time at Milazzo; then, on a rickety rural train, I overshot the sanctuary's stop at Patti, a small seaside resort and reputed Mafia enclave. I returned on yet another train and, finally, luggage in hand, disembarked at the muggy station. I walked out of the station, hoping to find a bus to the sanctuary. A middle-aged man, leaning against a taxi, peered at me over a newspaper. We exchanged glances; he looked disconcertingly familiar. He continued staring as I walked by. I stopped, looking again at him. Then I realized it was the same taxi driver who had driven me to the sanctuary two years before: Remo Maniaci.

I had actually written down Remo's name in the notebook I still carried with me. He had been charming, charging little when he had taken us to the sanctuary and found it closed. When I had returned to the States I had even sent him a letter with a snapshot, showing him holding a plaster statue of the Black Madonna that I had bought—and subsequently dropped, its head falling off in the rush to the station—that evening. I laughed to myself, knowing he would remember me as the relentless *giornalista* with a thousand questions about the sanctuary and Madonna.

"Remo?"

He seemed to recognize me at the same instant, and his eyes lit up. He shook his head in disbelief.

"Remember . . . two years ago? I'm Susanna . . ."

"Of course!" he nodded, beaming and holding out his hand.

"Did you receive the picture?"

"Yes. *Grazie.* What are you doing here?"

"I'm in Trapani for Easter. But I have come to Tindari again to try to see the Black Madonna."

"*Bèllo*—the sanctuary is open today! I will take you there."

He practically drove the taxi off before I had closed the door. As if on remote control, the car cruised out of Patti toward the sanctuary. We smiled at each other, amused at the coincidental meeting. I was pleased; though gun-shy after my Syracuse experience, I judged Remo to be totally honorable. After all, anyone who was so fond of the sanctuary and who had explained its history so patiently when I had come before couldn't be all that bad. Of course, he wondered about my traveling alone. When the inevitable question came, as he slowed at a railroad crossing, he tried to sound casual.

"So you are traveling by yourself?"

"Yes, I'm on research." Since he knew that I was a writer and photographer, this explanation seemed to satisfy him; he nodded his head, then bumped the car over the crossing, and zoomed up the mountain road. Soon we were a thousand feet above Patti; we drove into a little valley and up again toward a distant rocky promontory.

A half-mile down from the sanctuary we passed a large group of pilgrims waving palm fronds as they walked up the road. A few vendors were out, selling items like sunglasses and cassette tapes. One stall mixed the sacred and profane, with paintings of eighteenth-century maidens and big-eyed children stacked next to baroque Madonnas. Finally, on the right, was the sanctuary, a large church housing the Madonna. Built in the 1970s, it was tall, constructed of pink stone; it looked new. I disliked it, thinking a Black Madonna should be housed in something earthy and archaic. But at least today it was open to visitors.

I got out of the taxi, asking Remo to meet me in time to make the 5:00 P.M. train for Palermo. He agreed and put my extra bags in his trunk. With just my camera and a journal, I set off.

Before entering the sanctuary, I walked across the parking lot to see the spectacular view. Going down a small stairway to a grassy knoll, I looked below me a thousand feet to the Tyrrhenian Sea. It surrounded the promontory on three sides. All along the bottom of the cliff, curving back to Patti, were white beaches inset with blue lakes; one, locals pointed out, was in the shape of a woman's body. I thought of the legend of Tindari's Black Madonna that sprang from this holy place.

About A.D. 1100—around the date when the original Madonna of Trapani had appeared—Tindari's Madonna had come by ship from an "unknown country" in the East. According to the legend, a horrific storm had forced the ship to seek shelter in the harbor below the promontory. But when the storm had ended and the sailors lifted anchor, the ship would not budge. The sailors lightened the ship's load, piece by piece. Still the ship would not move. At last, the box containing the strange statue was removed

Tambourines among a vendor's wares; Sanctuary of the Black Madonna, Tindari.

and brought to shore. The ship was now free, and the sailors realized that the Madonna herself had chosen Tindari as a resting place. They carried her up to a small medieval church, which had been built from the stones of a Greek temple and which stood on the top of the promontory where the sanctuary was now. I had seen the temple's stones when I had driven in with Remo—in fact, they were scattered all over the sanctuary grounds. What interested me was that this original temple had been dedicated to a Mother Goddess, Cybele. Originally from Anatolia, she had been worshiped in pre-Hellenic times as an important fertility goddess, predating Demeter and Persephone. Eventually a fertility cult to Cybele had spread throughout the Mediterranean and, in the Roman era, had been brought to Rome at the request of the highest priestess, the Cumaean Sibyl. The Black Madonna of Tindari had chosen an appropriate spot.

I watched the pilgrims carrying their palms into the sanctuary above me, remembering that Christianity's first official Easter rites were directly influenced by the cult of Cybele, which included the worship of her son-consort, Attis. As late as the third century A.D., the death and resurrection of Attis had been celebrated every spring in Rome at the equinox. Roman writers described public ceremonies, from March 15 to 27, where flagellants gashed themselves with knives, sprinkling their blood on the pine tree that symbolized Attis. The god's image was then laid on a bier and mourned by worshipers and his mother-lover, Cybele. But on March 25, the Hillaria, he was resurrected. And on the last day, Cybele was carried in procession. These rites were very similar to those of the Christian Holy Week; in fact, fourth-century A.D. pagan critics officially accused the early Catholic fathers of plagiarism.

Inanna, Attis, Adonis, Persephone, Osiris, Christ . . . I had found a growing list of dying and resurrecting deities. And the mourning goddesses, like a group of

Facade, Sanctuary of the Black Madonna; Tindari.

sisters, continued the list, with Cybele, Demeter, Isis, and the *Addolorata*. As I considered the Black Madonna waiting in the church above me, I wondered who she was in relationship to the deities I had found.

I climbed up to the sanctuary, looking up at the mosaic of the Black Madonna on the facade. Old women made the sign of the cross as they entered. Some pilgrims were on their knees; one family supported a crippled boy as they walked devoutly through the doors. I entered, too, and walked down the long dark nave. At the end, under a dome decorated with frescoes and mosaics of miracles attributed to the Madonna, was an ornate altar upon which bronze angels held up a tall, glass case. Inside this case was the Madonna, standing about four feet high. She was carved of ebony and wore a gold brocaded cape and ornate Byzantine crown, as did the child in her arms.

Her dark face was almost frightening as it gazed down at me. It looked shriveled up, as if unearthed from some ancient archaeological site. She was worlds removed from the *Madonna dei Trapani* or other sweet images of the Virgin. She looked stern and fearsome. What kind of prayers, I wondered, did one say to this woman?

I knelt down with the pilgrims. Several women were crying; one man had crawled on his knees all the way down the aisle. I wanted to get closer, to touch her. But like the *Santoni*, the Madonna was separated from me in her houselike glass case. Under her feet was written *"Nigra Sum"* . . . I Am Black. At least the Catholic church did not deny her origins. But what was blackness? And what did this blackness mean?

It seemed to be reflected in the faces of the pilgrims. They were not devotees preparing for a wedding or saying casual prayers. In awe of her, several cried as they kneeled on the hard marble floor and remembered the often-told legends about her—how thousands had been cured of sickness, how shipwrecked sailors had been brought safely to shore. How one woman, indignant after a month's pilgrimage to the sanctuary, had spat with scorn on seeing the Madonna's "Ethiopian" face. At the same moment her child, wandering away from her, had accidently fallen off the cliffs by the sanctuary and landed on the beach below. The woman, climbing down and finding the child miraculously alive, believed her to have been saved by the Madonna and the very darkness she had disavowed.

I looked closer at the Madonna; in her free hand was a large flowering stalk: I imagined it as the tree on which Attis had died. And under the throne was a white marble sculpture of the Last Supper with Christ, his chalice held high, transforming wine into blood—was this Attis's sacrifice? It was probably wishful thinking on my part. But whoever this Black Madonna was, these pilgrims had not come to worship the usual image of Mary in her female purity and loveliness.

As with those who prayed to the *Madonna Addolorata*, these people had come for solace, for relief from pain, and in gratitude. One woman, tears streaming down her face, held a pale, thin baby out to the Black Madonna. A man hobbled in on crutches, his face quivering as he looked at her. Another woman reached up to touch the Madonna's glass case, then rubbed her pregnant belly. A man came in, carrying a wheat stalk in his hand.

As a fertility symbol, the Black Madonna represented the mysteries of regeneration. To these pilgrims, she had seen everything: the life and death of crops, animals, people, and souls, for untold millennia. She was both Attis and Cybele, both Demeter and Persephone. In her fertility, she also had compassion. But she was not sorrowing or distraught. Nor was she sweet or demure. She just *was*, exuding power and self-assurance.

I wanted this self-knowledge, too. For me, looking into the Black Madonna's face was like gazing into the unknown. Yet I also recognized something there.

I had seen it in the photographs I had studied of immigrants to America. Surely they had faced an unknown. I remembered one I had saved from a *Life* magazine cover, of a mother and daughter at Ellis Island in New York. The mother had been younger than I, but she looked older, with deeply weathered lines on her forehead. How scruffy her shoes had been, telling of long walks on dusty roads. She could have been from Italy, or Turkey, or Czechoslovakia. It didn't matter: the shoes, the handmade clothes, the look formed a universal uniform. The woman had an upturned nose, swollen from the blustery New York weather for which she and her daughter, in threadbare coats, were ill prepared. Though the photographer's flash powder caught her looking timid, I had never forgotten how high she had held her head nor the almost naive hope that had blazed out of her large bright eyes.

I had seen this courage in my grandmother's face; sometimes I had even fantasized that she was a descendant of the matriarchal Amazon women warriors of ancient Scythia. They had been worshipers of Cybele. And, like the Amazons, Carolina was large, big-boned, and full-breasted. She, too, was an excellent horsewoman. I remembered the stories she had told me of how she had helped her family raise horses and how, to train them, she had ridden bareback through the surf along the Terracina beach. Women like my grandmother had a primitive strength in their blood. Were they all, at heart, Amazons . . . or Cybeles, Demeters, or Black Madonnas? But in a patriarchy and, especially in Carolina's loss of her roots by coming to America, they had forgotten the real depth of their power.

The woman next to me held out her child again; her older boy, about six, reached to comfort her. Somehow I believed the Madonna would answer their prayers.

Could this Madonna help me to regain my own power? To look into my own unknown, my own uncharted terrain? If this terrain, for my grandmother, had been a new country, for me it was a journey back to an old one. Ultimately, with this Madonna and my journey to Sicily, I seemed to look into the uncharted world of my own soul.

I left the sanctuary and, with the other pilgrims, felt strengthened. Now was the time, with them, to buy a memento of my visit. I went over to the booths that lined the square in front of the church. Every imaginable icon of the Madonna was for sale: holy cards, medals, plastic pictures, Madonnas turned into lamps, scapulars, etched drinking glasses, velvet paintings, seashells painted with her image, and even silver refrigerator magnets. There were votive necklaces made of orange-colored seedpods and guidebooks describing Tindari and the Madonna's miracles and legends. Since I had broken the plaster statue I had bought two years before, I found another one in a booth at the far end of the square. I splurged, spending almost $20; it was carved of stone and painted in intricate detail. Now I had an hour before Remo would arrive, and I decided to return to the sanctuary.

I passed around it to the back, hoping to look at its foundation; perhaps some of the original church's stones—and therefore those of Cybele's temple—were still in place. The stones on the very back, below me where the foundation joined the cliff face, were obscured by a railing, so I set my statue and bag down for a closer look. Just then, the sacristan came out a side door of the sanctuary and walked over. Worried that this area was off limits, I quickly explained my interest in the history of the original church. Did any of the foundation stones still remain?

"Yes, you can see a few," he said, pointing over the railing. I leaned over it as far as I could, seeing now that these stones looked old, hand-cut, and very different from the pink stones of the newer sanctuary. Were these Cybele's temple stones? Where were the others, I asked? The

Souvenir statues of the Black Madonna; vendor's shop, Tindari.

sacristan said he did not know, throwing up his hands in a helpless gesture.

This was a problem I had encountered before, looking for traces of archaeological remains in Italy and Sicily. I remembered how once, in Terracina, I had looked for the stones of the Appian Way, the Roman highway that had been built down the length of Italy and that cut right through my relatives' town. I had spent a day tracking them, following signs through side streets that had been marked "Via Appia." The streets had been paved over, but I had been determined to find just a few stones of the old Roman route. Surely something remained. I had asked at houses along the way, but the occupants had regarded me doubtfully. It was impossible, they said. They had not been interested; obviously a paved road through Terracina was far better than the bumpy highway of the Roman legionnaires. But I had persisted and had finally found them. A little boy had led me to them, right in front of his house. They had broken through the pavement; he had kicked at the dust and, like a subflooring, the huge smooth stones of the Via Appia had been visible underneath. I had felt the excitement of an archaeologist, uncovering a rare find. Now I wondered if Cybele's stones could be tracked elsewhere—perhaps they had even been incorporated into the old houses that dotted the hillside below the sanctuary.

I seemed always to want proof of things. I wanted to hold an original rock right in my hand.

Then the sacristan noticed my statue of the Madonna, sitting on the rock where I had left it.

"If you are interested in the history of this place, you must know something." He picked up the statue. "The Madonna in the sanctuary is not the original one."

"No?" I said, taken aback. "Then who is she?"

Just then Remo came dashing around the corner of the sanctuary. Where had I been? he wondered. He was out of breath, insisting that we had to leave immediately if I was to make the train in time. I looked at the sacristan and down at the remains of the old stones. But Remo grabbed my camera bag and took me by the elbow. The sacristan handed the statue to me.

"Where is the real Madonna then?" I asked the sacristan.

"She is there." He was pointing to the substructure of the sanctuary, where the old rocks were. I looked again and now noticed some old windows, covered with grills.

"Come on. We'll be late," said Remo, pulling me along. I looked back helplessly, but it was too late. The sacristan, like some phantom, had disappeared into the sanctuary.

Remo and I ran to his taxi and drove back down the road to Patti and the train station, only to find that I was early, not late, for the train to Palermo. I had been wrong about the time; the express train would leave for Palermo at 7:00 P.M. instead of 5:00. Now I was worried: I had hoped to stay in Palermo that night, and this late departure meant that the train would arrive there almost at midnight—not a good situation, for I didn't have hotel reservations. We went outside to a pay phone, and I attempted to call the Hotel Liguria, where I had stayed before. I couldn't get through, trying several times losing lire in the meter. I wondered about staying in Patti for the night and going on to Palermo in the morning. I thought of the "real" Madonna that the sacristan had told me about; if I stayed, perhaps I would have time to go back and see if I could get underneath the sanctuary and find her. I mentioned this plan to Remo, and he assured me he knew of several inexpensive hotels in Patti. We left the station and headed toward town.

But instead of going directly to Patti's center, Remo took a road that circled above the town. He looked over at me, smiling happily.

"I am glad you are staying for the night. Patti is a beautiful place . . . And now I can show you a beautiful view."

I looked at him uneasily.

"You must see the view at night. The islands in the distance . . . Stromboli and Lipari. We can come back, after you get your hotel, and see all the beautiful lights."

Were Remo's intentions now more than just platonic? I couldn't be sure. He had been so helpful, both two years before and this afternoon, yet now I felt uncomfortable. I didn't have the energy to deal with Remo and the "beautiful view," nor did I want to risk a repeat of my Syracuse experience.

To simplify matters, I asked Remo to take me back to the station, telling him I had reconsidered and that I really needed to get back to Palermo tonight.

"But you'll be getting to Palermo very late," he argued. "It's dangerous for a woman."

"I'll be all right," I assured him.

I must not have sounded convincing, for he looked at me with genuine concern. How could I explain that he was the reason for my change of plans?

He drove dejectedly back to the station. I bought a ticket, then he sat with me on a bench while I waited, still trying to dissuade me from going. It was a difficult situation. I actually liked this man, who could have been my father, and felt both saddened and angry at the futility of traveling alone in Sicily. Why couldn't Sicilian males take me seriously and forget their penchant, when in the company of unescorted women, for "beautiful views"? Finally, Remo was quiet, but he stayed dutifully beside me on the bench and held my new Madonna statue in his hands. The train arrived, breaking our silence. I got up to go; Remo followed behind with the statue. Once I was on the train and in a compartment, Remo held the Madonna up to the window.

"Now be careful of her," he cautioned. "This time at least her head isn't broken!"

I took the statue and thanked him; halfheartedly he accepted a small payment for the chauffeuring he had done.

His frowning face looked increasingly poignant as the train pulled out.

I thought again of the Madonna I was leaving. Had I even seen her? I tried to imagine the "real" statue, in the chamber to which the sacristan had pointed. Did she look like the one I had seen, the one before whom the pilgrims had cried? Was she standing in some dark corner, perhaps wrapped in plastic? Or maybe she was in a box, like the one she had arrived in almost a thousand years ago. Who knew—perhaps the statue of Cybele was in the mysterious chamber, too. My imagination went wild.

But I realized that it didn't matter which Madonna I had seen. For the pilgrims in the sanctuary it hadn't mattered. The statue they had looked at simply symbolized the sacred place that Tindari had been since the time of Cybele. They knew the legends and stories about the Madonna; they had seen the cures. Most of all, they had had the physical experience of the journey they had made to Tindari. Perhaps this was all we could ever really have: the experience, inside ourselves, of having tried to find the thing we longed for.

I sat back in my seat, relieved again to be in the quiet of a train compartment. I watched out the window as the train closely paralleled the stormy Tyrrhenian Sea; leaning out the window at some stops, I could almost feel the spray in my face. The train continued along the yellowish rocky headlands until, at Cefalú, we were only two hours from Palermo. I looked out the window at the brightly lit station. Night had come, and now I had to think out my plans for negotiating Palermo's dark streets and finding a hotel at midnight.

Palermo was a city to be cautious in at night, even when accompanied. Hustlers abounded at the station, and even residents avoided the dimly lit streets off the main Corso after 10:00 P.M. I remembered the first time I had stayed overnight in Palermo eight years before, listening to shouts and what had sounded like gunshots in the alley behind the hotel. A shooting? A drunken brawl? In the intervening years, I had learned to appreciate this edge of danger, whether real or imagined in Palermo. It was a rough but exciting city, punctuated by unbelievable traffic jams and an eclectic mixture of Moorish, Norman, and baroque architecture. But now, at the prospect of arriving at night alone, I felt apprehensive. My only option was to get a taxi at the station, go to the Hotel Liguria, and hope that there was a vacancy. If not, maybe the *signora* would let me sleep on the couch.

The train left the Cefalú station, and a couple joined me in my compartment. We started talking, and I discovered that they lived in France and had taken the train from Paris. The woman, whose name was Anna, had grown up in Palermo and, with her French husband, was returning home for Holy Week. When they heard about my situation, they seemed concerned that I was arriving with no hotel reservations.

"I'll tell you what," offered Anna. "We'll all go together in a taxi to the Hotel Liguria. It is close by the apartment where my parents live. Then, if there are no rooms, you can spend the night with us."

I was astonished at this offer of lodging to a complete stranger. As I had discovered before, it sometimes took years for Sicilians to bring someone home to visit their family, let alone stay the night. Perhaps, by living in France, Anna had learned a more spontaneous way of life. I thanked her, relieved at the invitation, though the prospect of staying in a strange apartment had its own awkwardness. An hour later the train rolled into Palermo; I watched as Anna fixed her hair and makeup, anticipating the reunion with her family.

At the station, I trailed behind Anna and her husband as she fell into the arms of a handsome white-haired papa and a robust mama. Anna introduced me and told them of my predicament. The parents glanced at each other, startled at their daughter's plans to bed a foreigner in their home, but said nothing. We all then pushed our way though the crowded station and found a taxi. The driver looked impatiently at the five of us and our pile of bags, but Anna's husband passed him a handful of lire. We climbed in and were off.

If I had been alone, the speeding ride down the Corso, infamous with Palermo taxi drivers, would have been unnerving. Instead, in the company of laughing strangers, it was fun. The taxi wheeled up to the Hotel Liguria, and I quickly ran inside. I was surprised to see the same white-haired *signora* from my prior visits at the desk. She was just as amazed to see me, and best of all, she had a room. I ran back down to tell Anna and her family. She and I quickly exchanged addresses for future reference, and the taxi tore off.

Back at the desk, the *signora*, shaking her head at my late-hour appearance, escorted me to the same room I had had before. She handed me some towels and softly closed the door. Inside I collapsed on the bed and then, surprisingly, found that I felt wide awake. I went back down the hall and past the frowning *signora* to the street. At a pizza restaurant next door, several waiters were cleaning up for the night. I ordered a small pizza to go, which they wrapped up Sicilian style in paper, and two beers. Once more I passed the *signora* on the way to my room. There, I sat at a little desk with my Black Madonna statue standing over the steaming pizza. I thought of the last few days, circling Sicily alone. It had been both hallowed and harrowing. I felt victorious, as though I were returning home from a war—or from a sojourn in the underworld. Now, crawling out on my own, I could see ahead the faint glimmer of spring.

CHAPTER IX

Clara's *Casa*

"YOU MUST BE SUSANNA. Come in . . . we've been expecting you."

An attractive Tunisian woman of about thirty opened the door as two rambunctious little boys appeared behind her, pushing to see who the visitor was.

"I'm Bubba, Clara's assistant. She had to go down to the restaurant, but she'll be right back."

It was Wednesday of Holy Week, the day I was to meet with Clara. Timing my arrival perfectly, I had left Palermo early that morning after having spent two days there visiting the archaeological museum and the Norman cathedral at Monreale. When my bus dropped me off at the Trapani station, I had walked past the shop windows and poster-covered buildings on New Town's busy boulevard and made my way to Via Agugliaro. Clara's apartment was on this tiny street dividing New and Old Town, only half a block from the promenade along Trapani's Tyrrhenian seafront. This was Trapani's windy side, and the doors to Clara's building had slammed behind me with a shattering thud. I had taken an elevator up to the seventh floor, com-

Dress display in Trapani store window.

ing out into a wide hallway with mahogany paneling and, at the end, a window with an impressive view of the sea.

Bubba now helped me stash my bags in the hallway, then motioned me into a big library-like living room where I sat down in a comfortable chair by a window. The two boys, about the same ages as mine, followed me with curiosity; the older one stood by the chair as the younger sat on its arm. They argued with each other over a drawing book that the little one had, which they both wanted to show me. The older one gave in to his brother and ran into another room, shortly returning with colored pencils and paper. He sprawled on the floor, drawing contentedly. The younger one flipped through the pages in his book, barraging me with questions as he explained his drawings; soon the older boy jumped up and joined us. I assumed they were Clara's children, although I hadn't known she had any. With their inquisitiveness, loudness, and the thousand things they had to ask or show me, they seemed atypical of Sicilian children, who were usually more reserved. After a while Bubba called them into the kitchen; apparently they had not finished their breakfast.

I sat back and studied the room. It was a large, high-ceilinged multipurpose room for visiting, eating, or reading. It reminded me of rooms described in Lampedusa's *The Leopard*; it could have been the nineteenth-century study of Prince Salina in his baronial estate. It had the feel of having been lived in for decades: comfortable antique furniture sat on the parquet floors; fine lithographs and paintings were on the walls. It had an unkempt quality, too, with posters tacked to the walls and the remains of a dead decorated Christmas tree, which looked more like a big branch, by the doorway. It was now almost April. Had Clara left it up intentionally, or had she been too busy to take it down? I could identify with either possibility; in the past, with my own Christmas trees, I had done both. At any rate, this untidy icon was also decidedly un-Sicilian.

But most atypical were the thousands of books lining the walls. It was a hefty collection for a young *signora*, even one with a Ph.D. I looked at some of the Italian authors and titles: Verga, Pirandello, Sciascia, modern Italian and Sicilian writers, all the classics including works on Shakespeare, ancient archaeology, mythology, and anthropology. There was a sizable collection of Sicilian fiction and poetry and works on Italian feminism. Many of the books were first editions and very old. I wondered if Clara had bought them all. Though my own library was not nearly as big, I felt right at home; I picked a few selections off the shelves and settled back to read.

Then the front door opened and Clara stood in the doorway. She was wearing jeans and clogs and carrying a shopping bag full of vegetables. Her boys ran up, the little one jumping into her arms, as she explained breathlessly that something had come up at the restaurant; ordinarily, this was her day off. Would I like some coffee? When I said yes, she ran into the kitchen and shortly returned with two cups. She pulled up another chair; flopping down in it, she kicked off her shoes, lit a cigarette, and looked expectantly at me.

"Tell me, how was your trip?" she asked.

I recounted my tales of the last week between sips of coffee, struggling to give her the sense, in my imperfect Italian, of what I had been up against while traveling around Sicily. She laughed at my story of the Syracuse near-abduction, nodding as if she had not for a second expected anything different.

"I told you life was difficult for women in Sicily!"

"Has it always been this way?"

"Not always. For instance, here in Trapani the men used to go out to fish for a year or more. The women lived alone, but they had each other . . . They went out, ran the stores and market, and became independent. When the men came home, they found the women running every-

Torn poster; Trapani.

thing. But now men don't go to sea for long periods, so the women have lost their power."

"But I have seen some women running things inside their homes."

"Yes, they have a power of sorts. But it's very hidden; it exists only inside." With stubby fingers she held her cigarette high while she thought for a moment. Then she put the cigarette out and got up to look for a book.

I thought of Carolina, living alone in Italy with three children while Antonio had gone ahead to America, and of the confident look she had had in that last photograph from Rome. When she came to America, she had left a rich support system behind. In America, immigrant women were worse off emotionally than their counterparts in Italy. In the new land, their own mothers had been left behind; there were no village healers, no magic herbs, and few miraculous statues or saints. Worse, in the New Jersey town where they lived, there had been no other Italians, except Antonio's uncle. Antonio himself had been illiterate. They had been very poor, and Carolina had stayed at home to run the family, knowing no other sympathetic women with whom she could commiserate or relieve her loneliness.

How ironic that the hearth had become the symbol of Carolina's isolation. In the time of the Mother Goddesses, the hearth had been the earliest social center, where women had reigned over religious matters. The life outside, where men hunted, fished, or defended territory, was not considered as important as this inner life. How different were the hearths that Grandmother, my mother, and I had experienced! To me, the home could easily become a trap. I remembered finally feeling "myself" when, after I was married, I had lived alone on several occasions: I had gone to a different state to attend graduate school; there, I could come and go as I pleased. I had my own rules, not those that others had defined for me. I knew how

Clara's fisher-wives must have felt: relishing their new independence, then having to change gears when the men returned.

"But what about the younger women in Sicily, are they changing?" I asked Clara, who was still searching through the bookshelves.

She turned around to look at me. "Not really . . . they don't know any other way. Look at the young girls in the procession—they only do it for show, or they dress as old women."

I thought of Angela Amoroso and of Patrizia. Even though Angela had a husband who was gone some of the time, she was, ironically, housebound. Perhaps the songs she had sung that afternoon were a sign that, somewhere deep inside, the old fires were still burning. But Patrizia was still a very traditional girl. I wondered what it would take for things to change in Trapani—another Trojan War?

"I want women to have a better life here, to get them out." Clara had found the book she was looking for and sat down by me again. "But, unfortunately, this is more the mode of the younger women," she said, handing the book to me.

It was a cartoon-style joke book, in Italian, about a competent though frazzled Italian woman trying to fill her various roles. One showed the woman as her husband came home from work, roses in hand. She stood in the kitchen wearing a bra and panties out of Frederick's of Hollywood, reading *The Happy Hooker* while expertly stirring spaghetti with one hand and feeding a baby in a nearby high chair; another toddler climbed at her feet, and a picture of the Virgin was on the wall.

This cartoon, in particular, said it all. But the woman in the drawing looked contented with her juggling act; she wasn't jaded yet. I wondered if she would have to be as old as Angela or Nina before she would resort to lewd songs.

Clara and I flipped through the pages, laughing. So

many of the cartoons were set in the kitchen, obviously the center of the woman's life. I asked Clara about her own cooking in the restaurant and how she had learned. I was surprised at her answer.

"My father. He loved to cook . . . but he also loved those books." She looked around admiringly at the bookshelves. "He thought I should be well-rounded, so he taught me to do everything: to cook and to be a scholar. He even taught me to repair radios!"

Clara's boys came in, their breakfast finished. She sat on the floor and they jumped all over her; our conversation was interrupted so she could look at their drawing book.

In a moment, she looked up. "You know, to change things here, we have to start with the children. That's what my father tried to do. He always said, 'One stone at a time to build a house.' "

Bubba now joined us, sitting on the floor with Clara and the boys. Our little group seemed international and reassuring. It was a relief to be around precocious kids, a restaurateur who repaired radios, and an African woman who was an "assistant," not a maid.

The phone rang and Clara answered it. It was someone at the restaurant; there were problems with the stove, and Clara had to go down again.

"Do you want to go with me?" Clara asked, putting on a jacket.

She suggested I leave my bags in the hallway; I was welcome to stay the rest of the week if I liked. In fact, she wondered, what were my plans in the next few days before the procession? I admitted that I wasn't sure but that I probably should check in with the Amorosos before I decided. Just then, a man about Clara's age came in the door, ready to drive us down. Clara introduced him as Angelo, her boyfriend; he lived here in the apartment and helped her with the restaurant. But I surmised that he was not the father of her children; tall and blond, he was from Genoa in northern Italy, and Clara said they had only known each other for a few years.

We crowded into Angelo's car and were soon at the restaurant. The boys sprawled at a table, drawing in their book while Bubba and I talked and Angelo and Clara worked on the stove in the back. I walked around the empty restaurant, looking at the paintings and photographs on the wall. Over the door to the kitchen, I noticed some ornate wreaths, angels, and birds made entirely of hardened bread. They were beautiful and obviously handmade.

"What are these?" I called in to Clara.

She looked at where I was pointing. "Those are *pane de San Giuseppe*," she said. "They are made by the women of Salemi every March nineteenth, Saint Joseph's feast day, and displayed on altars in the town."

The bread decorations were fascinating, their incredible curlicues and twisted shapes reminiscent of the details on Sicilian baroque churches. I realized that my arrival in Trapani from the States had coincided with the very day of the feast; if I had known about it, I told Clara, I would have tried to attend.

She thought a moment. "You can still see something similar, in San Biago Platani. The women there should be about ready to put up their *pane* all over the town. It is an Easter tradition."

"Where is San Biago Platani?" I asked. I hadn't heard of it.

"Outside of Agrigento, up in the mountains . . . Actually, you could go there now and still get back in time for the procession."

Although Agrigento was a long bus ride down the coast, it seemed like a good idea. In Agrigento were Sicily's finest Greek temples, and I wanted to revisit them. But since I had to leave for the States right after Easter, would I have time?

I knew there was a 1:00 bus every day to Agrigento; if this plan were to work, I would have to leave immediately.

Clara and Angelo seemed tied up with the restaurant, and really, I had little else to do. I decided to go and told Clara I would walk back to the apartment myself and get my bags.

"I don't think you'll regret it," said Clara, calling from somewhere behind the stove. "You will like the women of San Biago. But hurry back. Remember, we are walking with the *Ceto Salinai* together. Come back here, to the restaurant, before the procession begins on Friday."

A new plan was in place: two days in Agrigento and San Biago, and then the procession. I hugged Clara, Bubba, and the boys; these new friends had no quarrel with spontaneous decisions. I walked back to the apartment, got my bags, and hurried down to the station. I bought a ticket, then phoned the Amorosos to tell them of my plans. Fortunately, Patrizia answered; she sounded a little disappointed that I wasn't staying, but we agreed to see each other during the procession. Within moments, the bus had arrived, and I was heading south again, this time down the winding coast road.

CHAPTER X

Bread Ladies
of San Biago

THE BUS PULLED INTO Agrigento at 7:00 that night, a reasonable hour considering my last-minute decision and the other poorly planned expeditions I had made in Sicily. I felt queasy after the long ride and stopped for a soda in a restaurant close to the station. Then, looking at my guidebook, I walked to a tall hotel nearby that promised to provide a spectacular view of the Valley of the Temples below the town. Somewhat like Athens, Agrigento was perched on a hill, and its Doric temples were a mile below in the fertile belt of almond and lemon trees that lay between the city and the distant sea. Before, I had stayed in a hotel in the valley in order to be close to the temples; now lit from behind by the low-hanging sun, their amber-colored stonework was an impressive sight—the huge Concordia, the temple to Zeus, the familiar corner pediment of the temple to Castor and Pollux depicted on thousands of Sicilian postcards. Halfway up from the temples toward the town was the sanctuary dedicated to Demeter; like the *Santoni* at Palazzolo, it was separated from the main ruins. I hoped to visit it after I returned from San Biago; now, my first priority was to find a room for the night.

But when I went into the hotel I was surprised at the price. Fifty dollars a night was too much to pay, when I planned to be up at 5:00 A.M. to take a local bus to San Biago. Thinking I had plenty of time to look for something else, I headed for Agrigento's center.

I cut across a little piazza full of old men reading newspapers or playing bocce ball. Up the narrow Via Atena, I walked against the stream of evening strollers who were moving toward the piazza. Where were the hotels? I consulted my guidebook; for a tourist town there were few listings, and most were down in the valley by the temples. I found one in a side street but it was fully booked. It was getting dark, and I thought of returning to the expensive hotel by the station. Then I saw a small pensione sign, pointing down a flight of broken stone stairs to a small door at the bottom.

At the pensione's desk was a red-eyed man of about forty-five who was reading a Sicilian pulp paperback. He said he thought he had a room but, excusing himself, stated he wanted to check with "Mother." I looked around as he went into a nearby room. In the dimly lit foyer were two men playing cards at a dilapidated table. Across the foyer was an open doorway that led into the private quarters. This is where the desk clerk had gone; inside he was shaking awake a heavyset old woman who was sprawled in a rocking chair. He could barely wake her. She seemed sick, almost comatose; I noted that her feet, covered by huge slippers, were swollen to a pathetic size.

"Mama!" the desk clerk shouted again into her ear. Finally she stirred, and he whispered something to her. They seemed to be talking about my room. The desk clerk returned to the lobby. Yes, they could put me up for the night in their last remaining room, he said. It wasn't their best one, but would I like to see it?

We went to the room, down a short hallway from the foyer. It was quite a dismal place. The only contents were a lumpy bed and a small sink—but I would have to go without water, the desk clerk announced, as it had just been cut off that afternoon. He apologized that the room door did not have a key but pointed out that it did have a latch, albeit a flimsy one, on the inside.

The desk clerk looked at my camera bag. "I'd lock that up if I were you. I'll show you where." I followed as he plodded down the hallway and opened a door. Inside was a little cubicle, not much bigger than a closet. It had a bed, a few girlie posters on the wall, and some empty wine bottles stashed in a box. Apparently this was his room.

"I'll keep them here for the night," he offered.

We went back to my room. The whole situation seemed quite ludicrous, but I have always had a weakness for bargains, and when the man said I could have the room for $6, I said I would take it. After all, it would only be a few hours before I would leave to catch the bus.

Back at the desk, I paid the man and decided not to part with my camera bag. Reluctantly, I gave him the passport he requested. How would I get it back so early in the morning? He assured me that he would be up; all I need do was ring the buzzer on the desk. Warily, I left with my bags and walked downtown to look for a restaurant.

Holy Week was in full swing in Agrigento; lifelike Easter lambs made of hardened sugar sat coyly in little baskets in store windows amid the usual displays of fantastic marzipan fruit. I passed a church and looked inside to see candles sputtering in front of a statue of the sorrowing Madonna. At the end of the block I found a restaurant and, from a table by the window, I watched a procession pass by. A small brass band played a funeral march, followed by a group of solemn townspeople. Men held their hats to their chests; an old woman cried, dabbing a handkerchief to her eyes. At the end, six men carried a casket covered with flowers. They held the casket tenderly, swaying to the music's beat, just like the *portatori* who carried the sepulcher in Trapani's procession. The person in this casket, treated with the solemnity accorded the *Misteri* on Good Friday, could have been Christ: if one had to die, Holy Week seemed a good time to do it.

Inside the restaurant, I was the sole diner. The owner sat at a back table, tallying the day's receipts as a cook scraped the kitchen's grill. I put off returning to the hotel and lingered over a coffee; finally, at about 10:00 P.M., the owner hung a "Closed" sign in the door's window, and I paid my bill and left. The streets were now almost empty, and I walked quickly to the pensione.

Several Tunisian migrant workers had now joined the card-playing Sicilians, who were passing around bottles of wine. The door to the private quarters was closed. I wondered about the sick woman inside, as her obviously inebriated son weaved across the floor, garbled a slurred *buona notte* to me, and joined the men at the table. I tried to walk past their drunken stares as unobtrusively as possible and went directly to my room.

Once inside I fastened the latch and sat uneasily on the bed. I worried about getting my passport from the desk clerk in the morning, considering his present condition. Worse, I thought of the drinking men in the lobby and realized that, save the desk clerk's mother, I had not seen any other women around.

Was I the only female guest in the pensione?

I undressed, set my travel alarm, and lay in the clammy bed listening to the sounds of the men in the lobby. Their voices rose intermittently as they argued over the card game; soon there was a knock on the outside door of the pensione, followed by more loud voices. Others had arrived to join the party. Finally their voices quieted a little, and I managed to go to sleep.

At about 1:00 A.M., I was awakened by loud thumps and

the harsh voices of several men shouting at each other from the room next door. I got out of bed and stood with my ear to the wall. There was a loud crash, as if someone had thrown a piece of furniture against the wall, followed by the sound of breaking glass. The voices shouted again; then I heard a woman's harsh laugh. Where was I? Had I chanced into some drug den, or was this a red-light district?

There were more crashes. I checked the latch, then got dressed and sat on the bed. The shouting continued; I lay down again, still clothed. Although I knew I was in a dangerous situation, I felt strangely calm. I stayed wide awake, planning how I would bolt out the door to the balcony and make the short leap down into the street if anyone entered my room. At about 3:00 A.M. when the noises finally stopped, I fell asleep. An hour later, my alarm went off.

I picked up my bags and quietly opened the door. In the lobby several of the men were lying over each other, snoring loudly. Wine bottles and cards were strewn on the floor. I rang the buzzer, and miraculously, the desk clerk appeared within moments, plodding down the hallway. He looked a wreck, and his eyes avoided mine. Fumbling behind the desk, he mumbled *"Perdone me, signora,"* and finally set the passport on the counter.

Feeling groggy from no sleep, I walked in the dark down to the bus station and bought coffee in a just-opening café while the bus for San Biago warmed up. As I had with so many other Sicilian conveyances that had offered me respite, I gladly climbed on the bus and collapsed into a front seat. The driver headed inland out of Agrigento. In spite of the coffee, I promptly fell asleep.

I woke to behold a different world. It was raining, and we were high in the mountains above Agrigento. The driver stopped to let a farmer on. He was covered with a piece of plastic used as a raincoat, and he carried a sack of small artichokes, the delicious Sicilian *carciòfi*, glistening with drops of rain. He joked with the bus driver, whom he knew, then smiled at me and sat in the seat across the aisle. A mile farther on a woman got on, a small baby bundled in her shawl. She smiled at me, too, in country friendliness.

Soon the bus was full of peasants chatting good-naturedly. How good it felt to be among these mountain folk. Everywhere, in the blasts of cold air that shot through the bus's door at each stop or in the peasants' sweat and bags of vegetables, I could smell the wet earth. Fields of bright green wheat were interspersed like a checkerboard with plots of magenta wildflowers. In the drizzling rain and bank of mist, these gently rolling hills were like my grandmother's patchwork quilts, tucked up over the coastal plain far below us. My uncomfortable night in Agrigento was already a distant memory.

It was still raining when we arrived in San Biago, which perched near the top of Mount Cammarata. On the way, I had asked the bus driver about San Biago's "bread ladies," and now he helped me off the bus, put up an umbrella, and, taking my arm, escorted me across the puddle-filled piazza and around the corner to a side street. We entered a garagelike building where two women were making arch-shaped wooden frames. Could you take the *signora* to see the *pane?* the driver asked the women. They looked at me with curiosity, surprised that a foreigner had come to their town. Eager to help, one took off her apron. She pointed to a three-story building across the street.

"First you must see the paintings," she said.

She held a newspaper over her head as we dashed across to an open door. We climbed two flights of stairs, arriving at a landing off which was a door into a large storeroom. Inside, an older woman and a young girl were putting the final touches on what appeared to be religious paintings. They were about three feet high, on arch-

San Biago Platani.

shaped pieces of Plexiglas that, because of its transparency, gave the painting the appearance of stained glass.

"Here are Stella and Vincenza," said the woman. They smiled at me and continued their work. I could see that the paintings were mostly of Easter subjects: a sorrowing Christ crowned with thorns, a chalice, a Madonna painted in brilliant blue. But others included symbols of fertility worked into the Holy Week theme: stalks of wheat or a bowl of ripe grapes and leaves.

"These paintings will be put up on our main street," explained Stella. "Every year we make new ones . . . over there you can see our designs for last Easter." She pointed to a stack covered with plastic and leaning against the wall.

But where was the famed *pane?* I wondered. Perhaps Clara had been wrong. As if answering my silent question, Stella got up and put on a shawl.

"Come with me," she said, touching my elbow gently and steering me toward the stairs. Apparently she was to continue as my tour guide. We walked down the stairs to the street. It was still raining; I followed Stella as she dodged puddles, then turned up a muddy street.

We were now on San Biago's main street above the piazza. Arcing over the street and along the sides of buildings were wooden frames to which, Stella said, the paintings, tree boughs, and *pane* would be attached. Everyone in town was worried, she said, that the rain would spoil their plans to decorate tomorrow, on Good Friday. We turned into a winding street; in the downpour, we were the only ones about. I looked into a steam-filled bakery shop where two men in wool jackets and caps hovered over pastries and cups of anisette. Farther up the street a tiny old woman in a kerchief peered out from her doorway. Her mouth turned into a toothless grin.

"Buon giorno, signorina," she murmured, then cheerfully watched us as we trudged up the street.

At the top of the hill we stopped at another little building, which Stella unlocked. Inside were more wooden frames, boughs, and paintings from previous years. Still I saw no bread.

Across the road was a building that reminded me of an old school, with sturdy, metal-cased windows. We crossed a kind of parking lot and went up the back stairs. Stella put a key into the door's lock, then turned to look at me with a glimmer in her eye.

"And this," she said proudly, "is the *pane*."

She stood inside the door, stretching out her arms like a conductor calling forth an orchestra's first notes. I followed her in, feasting my eyes on a huge room full of hundreds of bread ornaments more fantastic even than those I had seen in Clara's restaurant. They were everywhere—on long tables, chairs, and newspapers on the floor. Flowers, birds, butterflies, angels, lambs, hearts, Madonnas, chalices, grape clusters, fruits, little churches, eggs: every imaginable icon related to the Easter season was here. They were of varying size; some were quite large and would be used as central motifs on the wooden arches. Stella pointed out a group that looked like decorative tiles, to be used as fanciful bread doors that would face each other on a central platform in the piazza. Each piece was crafted with fine precision: small bits of bread creating an angel's curling hair or appliquéd bread pieces making stained-glass windows on a little church. But mostly, Stella explained, the *pane* symbolized the bread used by Christ in the Last Supper.

News of my arrival seemed to spread through a kind of grapevine, and two more women soon arrived to help Stella with my tour. Stella introduced them as Santina and Angela; together they showed me mixing bowls of hardened sugar and water, an icing that would be painted on some of the *pane* as further decoration. Meanwhile, Stella fretted over one elaborate construction, a large church with scores of doves fluttering on the towers. Some of the birds had broken off and, mixing up a kind of sugared glue, she began to repair them. I watched awhile, then asked Stella how long the women of San Biago had been making *pane*.

She wrinkled her forehead in thought, as if she had never considered this question before.

"Oh, I think one or two hundred years. Or maybe longer. Who knows?"

Angela and Santina helped to repair the *pane* church, then tackled some other broken pieces. As they worked, they laughed and sang; I took a few photographs, and Stella got up and started clowning, holding two huge bread sheep at her waist in her strong hands.

"Baa . . . baa," she mimicked.

"Coo . . . coo," said Santina, joining Stella with two large doves in her hands. They walked down the rows of ornaments, looking for others to repair.

A feeling of solidarity with these women and their joyful rituals engulfed me as up and down the rows of *pane* they went. They reminded me, in a way, of Clara and the way she sauntered with aplomb around her restaurant.

In Stella's laugh, I heard my grandmother once more. Joking with her friends and dressed in a hand-knit sweater like those that Carolina used to wear, Stella looked and acted like my grandmother. Were these the kind of women that Carolina had left behind? Was this the life she might have had? Somehow Stella and her friends were different from the Amoroso women, from Lucia, and from most of the other Sicilian women I had met. Perhaps this was because I now saw them outside the confines of their homes. And unlike Trapani's women, they had taken charge of San Biago's Easter tradition. It was created entirely by women, and Stella and her friends seemed self-confident and free, like those former fisher-wives that Clara had told me about. I wondered, too, if their sense of power came directly from the material with which they worked: the *pane*.

Santina Pastorella decorates the pane *of San Biago.*

In the rows of bread, Stella pointed out her favorites to me. The rain had stopped. A shaft of sunlight streamed through the window and seemed to illuminate almost purposefully an exquisite bread chalice with tiny grape leaves, also made of bread, winding around it. Stella picked up the piece, holding it carefully to inspect it for cracks. The light glowed around Stella and the chalice; instead of a Last Supper, I felt I was watching a priestess in an ancient fertility rite. Her bread offering was like the ritual cakes the women had brought to the old sanctuaries of Demeter and Persephone.

Stella set the chalice down, satisfied that it was intact, and turned to me.

"The women are having a meeting in a little while, about the decorating tomorrow. Would you like to come?"

I wanted to but knew I couldn't. It was now noon and at 1:00 P.M. I had to catch the only bus back to Agrigento if I was going to leave for Trapani early the next morning. I cursed my hurried schedule, wishing I had come to San Biago before. How wonderful it would be to stay in this mountain town, experiencing Easter with these women and their bread. I told Stella I would try to return for another Easter and see San Biago's rituals from start to finish. This pleased her immensely.

"Then maybe you would like to take a *pane* home with you?" suggested Stella. "Please, find one you like."

There were so many; it was difficult to choose, and I didn't want to take one that was too important. Stella, sensing my dilemma, helped me look.

"Here is one I like very much," said Stella, finally picking one up.

It was a beautiful butterfly. Though small, it was handsomely crafted with tiny antennae and Monarch-like patterns made with appliquéd bread pieces. I accepted it gratefully; it was a perfect symbol for how I felt, now that I had visited San Biago. Here on this mountaintop, I had found a safe and nurturing place, and meeting these women, who had retained their power through this simple ritual of bread, I felt a metamorphosis occurring deep within me. Like the butterfly, my own wings were dry now and ready for flight.

Stella wrapped my butterfly in a newspaper; then, she, Angela, and Santina covered the bowls of glue, put on their shawls, and escorted me out.

I told Stella that I would like to say good-bye to Vincenza and see the paintings one more time; the women led me back to the upstairs storeroom. Anxious not to miss their meeting, they told me I could go up by myself.

"Buona Pasqua," said Stella, wishing me a happy Easter as she hurried down the street. "We will wait for you to come back someday!"

I hurried up the stairs; the door was open, but Vincenza was not there, and the paints and brushes had been put away. Perhaps she had gone to the meeting, too. I stood in the middle of the room, admiring the paintings stacked around me. By the window was a beautiful Madonna, black lines painted around the figure to heighten the effect of stained glass. I walked quietly around the room, glad for this chance to look closely at the artwork on my own. Against the wall I spotted the stack of paintings from last Easter that Stella had mentioned before. They had been done on large boards instead of Plexiglas and seemed different in style from this year's paintings. I lifted one corner of their plastic covering for a closer look. There were only two of them, it turned out. The first painting was shaped like an arch about five feet high; its subject was the Pietà. In an elongated, almost El Greco, style someone had painted a sorrowing Mary holding a large Christ, covered in a pink robe, in her lap. I moved aside this first painting to look at the second—and caught my breath. Completed in the same style as the first, it was a painting of a Greek goddess! The board was in the shape of a circle; the goddess was dressed in a Greek toga, and one of her breasts was bared. In one hand, she held a loaf of bread. I had seen hundreds of terra-cottas like this in the archaeological museums in both Agrigento and Palermo. I was sure that this was a painting of Demeter.

I felt as if I had returned to the Enna church and found the statue of Demeter and Persephone magically restored to the altar. These San Biago women, with their paintings and bread, had not forgotten the old grain goddess. In one picture, they had painted the dead Christ in his mother's arms. But in the other, they had painted the resurrection: the new life symbolized by Demeter and her gift of bread.

I wanted to run, find Stella, and discuss my discovery with her. Wrapping the paintings back up, I hurried down the stairs to the street. The rain had begun again, and no one was around; then I realized I had no idea where Stella had gone. I walked up to the school building where the *pane* was. It was empty; then I ran back to the first building where the women had been making the frames. It was locked. I even went to the bakery; the two men were still sitting inside. Yes, they knew Stella and the women who made the *pane*, but who knew where their meeting might be?

It was close to 1:00; disappointed, I returned to the station to board the bus for Agrigento. I watched out the window as the driver wheeled through the empty streets. Soon we were on the highway, heading down the mountain. I unwrapped the bread butterfly that Stella had given me; this icon would have to sustain me until I could return.

Ironically, when I arrived in Agrigento that afternoon and walked down to Demeter's rock sanctuary, I found a medieval church there named San Biago, built on top of a fifth-century B.C. temple dedicated to the goddess. I could still see the temple's foundations and a round, flat altar stone where the offerings to Demeter and Persephone had been made. Below the church, dug into a cliff, was the rock sanctuary itself. Like the sanctuary of the *Santoni* at Palaz-zolo, it was a little-visited place. A white-haired custodian opened a gate and led me to the entrance of one of the tun-nels cut into the rock. Here, said the custodian, mysterious rituals honoring Demeter and Persephone had been per-formed. I ventured into the dark tunnel, with the custodian following after. Like the Levanzo cave, it was dark and musty, but at its end nothing remained of the original altar. There was no trace here of Queen Persephone or her mother.

Still, I was satisfied with the memory of what I had seen in San Biago. There I had finally found Demeter in the painting I had discovered and in the modern ritual of *pane*. Through their recipes, the "bread ladies" of San Biago were keeping a link to their foremothers of the ancient past. They offered an interesting counterpoint to Clara, who was creating a new recipe for the women of the future.

Tomorrow I would take the early-morning bus back to Trapani to meet with Clara just as the procession would be-gin. What mysteries, I wondered, would unfold in that coming night?

CHAPTER XI

Processione

IT WAS 3:00 A.M. in the middle of the night of the procession, and I had been following the *portatori* of the *Ceto Salinai* alone for almost three hours. There wasn't another woman in sight, just hundreds of men. Even the old women who followed the last platform had gone home to sleep.

The *Ceto Salinai* creaked and groaned, twisted and squeaked as the porters carried it another block, then bent their knees to put it down. They unwrapped their arms from the platform's long wooden poles, lit cigarettes, and passed around a thermos of hot coffee, which they poured into little cups. One older carrier peered at me with curiosity, then looked around at the other men. He knew that I was a friend of Clara's. So why was I still here when she had gone home?

Clara had been waiting for me when I had arrived in Trapani at 3:00 P.M. on Good Friday, after struggling through a frustrating traffic jam. We had gone out with Bubba and the children for a few hours to watch the procession, stopping in a bar on the way to offer toasts with glasses of sweet Averna.

"Susanna," she had said, "we must take back our power. To *potenza.*" She had raised her glass to mine.

"*Potenza,*" I repeated. "It is even a feminine word!"

Then she had returned to the restaurant, now crowded with out-of-towners. I had followed the *Misteri* alone, talking briefly with Carlo and Giuseppe, who luckily were so engrossed with their *ceti* that they had not asked me about my whereabouts during the past week. I had followed the Madonna's platform, too, but had not seen Angela and Patrizia among the candle-lit faces there. Back in the restaurant at 10:00 P.M., I had seen that Clara was still busy, but that Gian Carlo had arrived from Palermo. He was eager to carry again for the *Ceto Navanganti* — the seafarer's team — telling me that "every year, I'm never sure if I will." We left and followed this platform for several blocks; then, in a dramatic moment, Gian Carlo finally decided to make his move. He donned his *portatore* smock, ducked under the platform's poles, and vanished down the dark street.

At midnight I had met Clara at the *Ceto Salinai* on New Town's big boulevard. We had followed together for an hour. She had talked with the porters at rest stops, but, for some reason, she also seemed hesitant to carry. Then, after I had run down the darkened street to buy some coffee for us, I returned to the *Ceto Salinai* to find Clara gone.

A part of me assumed she would come back. Another part wondered if she hadn't had some secret intention in abandoning me like this. By now, I felt quite brave. It was exciting, walking alone beside the *portatori.* Despite the disapproving stares of the old women who passed by, I had come to a turning point in the last hour: I had resolved to follow the procession to its finish. Now I was one of only a few stragglers still following the *Misteri.*

The cool night air blew in from the sea. I shivered, mesmerized by the sights and sounds around me. Perhaps it was the lack of sleep or the heady smell of candle smoke that cast this spell—or the sight of the straining men working together, the creak of the old platform, the childlike thrill of being out all night, or perhaps it was the statue on the *Ceto Salinai* itself. The platform bore the figure of the Madonna holding the dead Christ in her arms, an image that always reminded me of my grandmother. I looked at the tired porters shouldering their burden. Suddenly, something pulled on me: it was as if I had no choice; I no longer wanted only to walk along like this, as an observer. I wanted to carry.

But without Clara, I wondered if I had a chance.

"These guys, they no know nothin'!" commented a carrier from the platform just behind the *Ceto Salinai.* He introduced himself as Nino. Several platforms, including mine, had stopped along a narrow street near the tip of Old Town. Nino, eager to speak to an American, continued in his broken English. He said he was a transplanted Sicilian living in Florida, where he had a contracting business. He told me with pride that he returned every year for the procession. But I was a little embarrassed by Nino's loudness, by how he called attention to himself with the dark glasses and black leather jacket he wore over his *portatore* smock.

"Now watch! They think because I talk to you we gonna run off and make love." He laughed, looking around at the men milling about their platforms and watching us. He downed his thick, syrupy coffee, then yelled something in Sicilian to one of them.

What did they think of him, let alone of me? He lived— and had achieved success—in America; therefore, he commanded a certain respect. Yet he acted like a gangster, portraying the mafioso image that the Sicilians disliked. He seemed to feel antagonistic toward them, or superior because he had left the old country behind. But however he

Madonna Addolorata *(Sorrowing Mother); detail, wall plaque.*

behaved, he was redeemed by the fact that he came back, every year, at Eastertime.

"But, geez . . . I do love this town," Nino blurted out, laughing and waving at another group of men across the piazza. Beneath his rough exterior, I could see he was simpatico.

"I want to carry," I suddenly announced.

He looked at me. "You crazy? You want to carry?"

"Yes, I do."

He considered my request for a moment.

"Well . . . you let me talk to my boss. I fix things for you." He looked at his watch. "When the bands come back, and it is dawn. You wait."

There wasn't much time before the bands would return and the entire procession would begin its reentry into the church. Without Clara there, I thought it presumptuous to ask if I could carry the *Salinai*. But with Nino's intercession, maybe I could help carry his *ceto*.

"*Al posto!* To your posts!" A *cònsole* shouted the command and snapped the *cioccola*. The carriers of the *Salinai* ran to their posts, lifting the huge weight onto their shoulders. Nino ran off to join his team of porters at the end of the street. Then the procession took off again.

I hurried to catch up. Like frenetic fireflies, the candles on the long line of platforms bobbed up and down, illuminating the tired faces of the porters. Eventually, we turned a corner, and the *Ceto Salinai* arrived at a large square by the boat harbor. The square was already jampacked with the other platforms and hordes of men. It was 5:00 A.M. Now commenced the hourlong wait for dawn.

I stood quietly, watching the men of the *Salinai* gather and lean against their *ceto*. They were a quiet group, their seriousness a contrast to the merrymaking of the other carriers. I scanned the boat harbor and the Tyrrhenian Sea beyond. It was no longer black but cerulean blue. Dawn

Lifting up the ceto; *Procession of the Mysteries, Trapani.*

would soon break; something had to happen soon if I was going to carry.

Nino returned, a look of disgust on his face. "I am sorry, Susanna. I talk to the boss. He says no woman can carry his *ceto*. I try! I no know what you canna do."

"Can't you plead with him again?" I begged. I could see Nino's *cònsole* across the square, watching us and frowning. It was hopeless.

The bands were arriving now; everyone was getting ready to leave the square. Exhausted men, half-delirious after so many hours with no sleep, ran to rejoin their teams once more.

Nino pulled off his black leather jacket, knowing that he would soon carry down the broad avenue where thousands of people would be watching.

"*Al posto!*" called Nino's *cònsole*.

"I must go. I am sorry!" shouted Nino as he raced away.

I ran back to the *Salinai* where the men, shouting directions to each other, were maneuvering the platform with its statues into position on a side street. Around the corner was the Corso. In moments it would be our turn to enter it. It was almost too late to ask to carry. With so many people watching, it would be too obvious for an *americana* suddenly to join the team. I tried to let go of my desire to carry; after all, what else did I have to prove in Sicily? I had discovered other things in the past few weeks. Was it not enough to have traveled alone? To have overcome my fears? I had found Demeter in San Biago; in fact, I had discovered traces of her throughout the island. I had my Black Madonna; I had my bread butterfly. I had begun a friendship with Clara. I had seen the *Santoni*, and I had met Stella. Through her, I had had a vision of my grandmother's original spirit.

I had gone a step further, too. With the procession, I had walked alone the entire night.

The *Ceto Salinai* turned onto the Corso. Several old

women watched me—an oddity, surely, in a long skirt, a bright yellow T-shirt covered by my baggy green sweater, and a purple headband—as I walked alongside the platform. But now I sensed that they accepted me as a familiar and relentless Trapani fixture. Smiling, they seemed to know at least that the *americana* had a devotion for the *Misteri*. In fact, we were now walking past the Amorosos' apartment on the Corso, and I recognized some of these waving older women as Angela and Patrizia's neighbors.

After a long rest stop, the band of the *Salinai* began a Lombardi march, the signal for the carriers to begin the *annacata*.

"*Al posto!*" called the *cònsole*.

It was a moment of high tension as the men picked up the *ceto* and began the first official steps of the long *entrata*. Excitement filled the air as the men started dancing, cutting a path through the scrambling crowd. My heart skipped a beat and tears came to my eyes at the sight: the carriers on this team were mostly older men, and it moved me to see them waltz together like this. It was an androgynous blend of strength and grace.

The oldest *portatore*, the one who had peered, so puzzled, at me before, glanced in my direction as he danced along on the front right pole of the platform. I smiled back at him, applauding his *annacata*. And then an astonishing thing happened: he gently pushed the porter in front of him forward a bit, and looking over at me, he pointed to his shoulder and the now-empty space on the pole. Again he pointed to his shoulder and to the empty space. He was asking me to carry.

I was stunned.

With a huge grin, I nodded my head. Quickly, so as not to cause the *portatori* to break step, I squeezed under the pole. The old porter and the man in front of him moved to give me more room. I brought my shoulder up to meet the pole, put my left arm around the arm of the porter beside me on the other pole, and stepped out with my right foot to the music's beat.

I was now moving with the men. It was like a dream: finally, I was carrying the *ceto*.

The first steps were awkward. The older men behind me nodded encouragement; the others, surprised at the newcomer, watched me a little doubtfully. With my right foot, I stepped on the heel of the *portatore* in front, and then, with my left, I caught the toes of the *portatore* to the left. I closed my eyes to concentrate; it was surprising to discover that the secret of carrying did not lie in physical strength or force, as I had thought. With sixteen people carrying, the weight of the platform could be handled easily. But to make it move with grace, one needed coordination and balance. It was necessary to dance together, as a group.

My technique improved. After about fifteen minutes, the *cònsole* signaled; we stopped the dance steps, hopped a few steps farther out of sheer inertia, then bent our knees to set the *ceto* down. Some of the carriers ducked outside the poles to take a rest. I stayed inside, feeling euphoric, surrounded by these wonderful men. All I could do was grin. The men smiled back at me; some were surprised at the old porter's invitation, and one or two eyebrows were raised, as if questioning whether my participation was an asset to the *ceto* or a liability. But most of them seemed quite matter-of-fact.

"Does it hurt?" asked one of them, indicating my shoulder.

I shook my head, trying to assure him that I felt fine. Another offered me a drink of water from a jug kept under the skirt of the *ceto*. I looked out at the crowd around us, watching me in this group of men. I wanted to show how reverent and serious I felt. The *portatori* treated me respectfully, as an equal. I wondered if I would be allowed to continue to carry; perhaps the older man's offer had only been a token gesture. Had he felt sorry for me, noticing how

Portatori *carry their heavy loads; Procession of the Mysteries, Trapani.*

long I had been following them? After all, only Clara had carried for them before, and she was from Trapani. Would these men allow an *americana* to carry the platform all the way down the Corso, under the probing eyes of the tradition-minded townspeople?

The *cònsole* snapped the *cioccola*, and the men got into position again under the poles. I looked at him; he was the one who would decide. He glanced in my direction, considered a moment, then nodded his head.

I was on.

The music started up again and we were off. This time, I performed the foot movements almost perfectly, neatly angling out my feet between those of the *portatori* in front and in back of me. It was exhilarating; I felt we were floating on some primal sea. We swayed our *ceto* from side to side; it was like a ship. Looking above me at the bobbing statue of the dead Christ in Mary's arms, I thought of Vikings rowing a slain warrior out to sea, of Phoenicians rowing their stately *corvi*. But now instead of just watching from the shore as their women would have done, I was in the midst of the movement.

The bright morning sun grew hotter as we made our way down the Corso. There were two or three more rest stops; at one of them I took off my sweater, and a porter stashed it under the platform's skirt for me. Soon we were in the heart of the Corso. The crowd, four and five people deep, stared at me as, mesmerized, I concentrated with the men. Women, clutching their husbands' arms, were startled as I came along. Then, when they saw my coordination and resolution they nodded, ever so subtly, in approval. A group of younger women watched me carefully, nudging each other; one walked out into the street for a closer look. As I passed by, they clapped and shouted in encouragement.

At first I was uneasy with the stares, as we approached the archbishop's palace, next to the San Lorenzo cathedral near the end of the Corso, where the archbishop stood on a balcony inspecting each *ceto* as it passed. This was an important test. I concentrated with all my might as we danced in place; like the other *portatori*, I held my head high and gazed straight ahead. Now, as the crowd stared at me, I looked right through them. But I wasn't playing a role; I had entered the trancelike state that I had observed in the carriers in previous processions.

We set the platform down in front of the archbishop, and the *portatori* patted my shoulder excitedly. The *còsole* beamed. They were all impressed. If the offer had been a token gesture at first, they now wanted me there. I was carrying it well. Now I suspected I might be offered the ultimate honor of bringing the *ceto* back into the church.

But was I capable of it? Never in my wildest imagination had I dreamed that they—the townspeople, everyone—would allow this. The *entrata*, the culmination of the procession, was a sacred act that thousands of people watched. The waltz had to be performed exactly right, the platform turned, the timing perfect. I was satisfied to stop now; I had carried for almost three hours. And the last thing I wanted was to stumble with the waltz steps, embarrassing the *portatori* and myself.

But again I had no choice. The band started the funeral dirge called *"Vela,"* the *cioccola* snapped again, and the *còsole* motioned me back under the poles. The men looked at me, then at each other. We were all becoming apprehensive now; from where we stood, we could see Via Tintori, the side street to the right angling off the Corso, which led around to the little piazza in front of the Church of the Purgatory. The narrow street was thick with people; they looked like phantoms in the haze of candle smoke. I positioned my elbow, clutched the arm of the carrier beside me, and pushed up on the pole.

The strains of *"Vela"* guided us as we made our way carefully around the corner and onto Via Tintori. We waltzed through the block-long street. Suddenly, I saw Patrizia and Angela in the crowd. They didn't see me until our *ceto* reached them; then Patrizia's mouth dropped open in disbelief. She grabbed Angela's arm, who watched in astonishment. They looked up and down my dancing form, as my black skirt, now coated with candle wax, swayed back and forth among the blue tunics of the *portatori*. I smiled at them, and as our *ceto* passed, they broke into broad grins.

At the end of the street we turned again to the right. Directly ahead of me, about a block away, was the little piazza and the church. We set the platform down for a last rest. Ahead of us, I could see the sixteenth statue group, depicting Christ crucified on the cross. It was already in the piazza, surrounded by the clamoring crowd, and its porters were dancing toward the ramp that led up into the church. Directly in front of us was the seventeenth group, *La Deposizione*, whose statues showed Christ being taken off the cross. I watched as the sixteenth *ceto* went up the ramp several times and finally entered the church. Then the seventeenth took off and danced into the piazza; we walked our platform a few yards forward into position. I was almost overcome with excitement; standing resolutely with the other carriers, I silently watched *La Deposizione* enter. People in the crowd nearby kept their eyes on us, realizing that a foreigner would now help take one of the *Misteri* into the church. I only hoped I would not disappoint them.

La Deposizione was in; we were next. The *cònsole* whispered to our band leader, who fluttered through his sheaf of music. Then the musicians put their instruments to their mouths, and the drummer sounded an ominous beat. The *cònsole* held his *cioccola* in the air, waiting for the music; we all waited, knowing how important the choice of the *entrata* song was. The first strains began and I was overjoyed: it was "Povero Fiore."

The *cònsole* snapped the *cioccola* and we got into position. I took a deep breath; then, with the men, we slowly raised the platform and headed the last remaining yards into the piazza. Hundreds of people followed along beside us; photographers came up to snap pictures of our faces and feet, and a television cameraman, stationed on a platform in the piazza, zoomed his telephoto lens our way. I closed my eyes, concentrating on the rhythm of the swaying forms around me.

We were now in front of the ramp. I felt my way with my feet as we turned the *ceto* almost a full circle, positioning ourselves to go backward up the ramp and into the church. The crowd was silent, watching us perform the difficult movement. Then we headed up the ramp for our first pass into the doors. This, I knew, was the big emotional moment for the *portatori* and the crowd; after the long procession together, everyone wanted the finale to last as long as possible. One or two passes, up and down the ramp, were considered too few; three or four were usual. Any more and the church officials stopped it, considering the prolongation a pagan display. We went up the ramp, then down again, our *cònsole* pushing on the poles to keep us from slipping. "*Povero Fiore*" resounded as we danced in place, then went up the ramp again. We paused, then came down. The crowd began to clap wildly as the *cònsole* steadied us at the bottom of the ramp for a third pass. I was overwhelmed and on the verge of tears. I looked out quickly through the men's arms around me and saw Carlo Sugameli and Giuseppe standing beside the ramp. They had already brought their platforms in. Carlo, his arm around Giuseppe, nodded his head gently. Giuseppe, a look of deep understanding on his face, simply gazed at me. His eyes were wet; a single tear ran down his cheek.

We went up the ramp a third time, then down again. Excited, the *cònsole* steadied the *ceto*; the murmuring crowd continued clapping as we went up again. But we didn't go in the doors; the crowd, excited now, held its breath as we paused. With the men, I felt ecstatic; with them, I didn't want our dance to end. We came back down, the crowd cheering us on to a fifth pass. Exhausted yet newly energized, we danced up again.

"Bravo!" cheered the crowd. They clapped wildly. We paused at the door again. Our *cònsole* hung onto the poles. Dark-suited officials, behind the *cònsole*, tried to push us in. But the *cònsole* and we *portatori* pushed in the opposite direction to the crowd's claps and encouragement. It was unbelievable but without breaking step, we waltzed down the ramp again. At this moment, I was transported. Surrounded by the men and the crowd, I was in a sacred world transcending time and place.

I had become the Goddess I had sought. And it seemed right and proper that she had rejoined the world of men. By joining these men, I felt I had given them, too, a new strength. With the *portatori*, I cried. I could hear their sobs around me, so beautiful, in the discovery of our newfound strength. I cried for so many things, not least of all for my own journey's end. But these were tears I had never experienced before. They were not the tears of Carolina, of mourning, or the tears shed onto sad pictures put in a woman's grave. They were the tears of the joyous Black Madonna, of Cybele, of *L'Addolorata*, of the thankful Demeter having found her daughter again. I, too, had found the lost part of myself. Together with the dancing men, I gladly waltzed up the ramp. We paused one last time. Then, unafraid of what I would find inside, I entered the doors and came home.

ACKNOWLEDGMENTS

I would like to thank my father for giving me my Italian American heritage, and Tom, Sky, and Shane Lloyd for their support. I owe gratitude to my special mentor, Robert Kostka; he has offered me inspiration and encouragement. I would also like to thank my agent, Natasha Kern, and Barbara Corrado Pope, Elizabeth Lyon, and Carol Bonomo Ahearn for their friendship and enthusiasm. Nancy Palmer Jones and Dorothy Wall are to be commended for their fine editing skills. Lastly, I am indebted to the generous people of Trapani, Sicily, without whom this book would not have been possible.

Photo: Kathy Hollis Cooper

About the Author

"Photographing the Christ *santos* in the churches of Mexico, Peru, and Ecuador, I became intrigued by the pre-Christian references I saw there: strange amulets hanging from the *santos'* wrists, or sheaves of corn brought to the churches on Good Friday. Then, in Italy, I attended the Good Friday Procession of the Mysteries in Trapani, Sicily, and saw the *Madonna Addolorata*. It was the recognition of this dark-skinned goddess, a role model of power for women, that became the nucleus for *No Pictures in My Grave*."

SUSAN CAPERNA LLOYD has a B.S. degree in art education and English, and an M.F.A. in photography, both from the University of Oregon. She teaches photography but devotes most of her time to writing, research traveling, and producing documentary films. Lloyd's writing and photography on Sicily have appeared in many magazines, and her documentary film about the Procession of the Mysteries in Trapani, *Processione: A Sicilian Easter,* has won numerous awards. Lloyd is currently working on a film about a Buddhist pilgrimage on the Japanese island of Shikoku. She lives in Jacksonville, Oregon, with her husband and two sons.